St. Francis
and the
Foolishness of God

*Your own journey clearly
reflects the values of
Francis and Clare —
adelante!
Marie Dennis*

ST. FRANCIS
AND THE
FOOLISHNESS OF GOD

Marie Dennis
Cynthia Moe-Lobeda
Joseph Nangle, O.F.M.
Stuart Taylor

ORBIS BOOKS

Maryknoll, New York 10545

Seventeenth Printing, October 2009

The Catholic Foreign Mission Society of America (Maryknoll) recruits and trains people for overseas missionary service. Through Orbis Books, Maryknoll aims to foster the international dialogue that is essential to mission. The books published, however, reflect the opinions of their authors and are not meant to represent the official position of the society.

Acknowledgment is gratefully extended for permission to reprint the following:

Saint Francis: A Model for Human Liberation by Leonardo Boff. English translation copyright © 1982 by The Crossroad Publishing Company. Reprinted by permission of The Crossroad Publishing Company. *The Canticle of Creatures: Symbols of Union* by Eloi Leclerc; *St. Francis of Assisi* by Raoul Manselli; and *St. Francis of Assisi: Writings and Early Biographies*, Marion Habig, ed., published by Franciscan Herald Press. Reprinted by permission of Franciscan Press. *The Little Flowers of St. Francis* by Raphael Brown, ed. and *St. Francis of Assisi* by Johannes Jörgensen published by Image Books. Reprinted with permission of Doubleday Books. Jack G. Shaheen, "Our Cultural Demon – the 'Ugly' Arab," *The Washington Post*, Outlook Section, August 19, 1990. Reprinted with permission of Jack G. Shaheen. *Keeping and Healing the Creation*, a Resource Paper prepared by The Presbyterian Eco-Justice Task Force, issued by the Committee on Social Witness Policy, Presbyterian Church (U.S.A.), 1989. Reprinted with permission.

Published by Orbis Books, Maryknoll, NY 10545
Manufactured in the United States of America

Biblical translations are from *The New American Bible*, *The New Jerusalem Bible*, and *The New Revised Standard Version*.

Library of Congress Cataloging-in-Publication Data

St. Francis and the foolishness of God / Marie Dennis . . . [et al.].
   p. cm.
   Includes bibliographical references.
   ISBN 0-88344-899-8 (pbk.)
   1. Francis, of Assisi, Saint, 1182-1226. 2. Spiritual life –
Christianity – Meditations. 3. Church and social problems –
Meditations. 4. Social justice. I. Dennis, Marie. II. Title:
Saint Francis and the foolishness of God.
BX4700.F6S6563 1993
271'.302 – dc20
                                                93-28727
                                                 CIP

Contents

v

Introduction

Narrative Theology

Throughout the history of the Franciscan community, whenever there has been a crisis, a shaking of the foundations in church and society, a new story of Francis has emerged. As each historical crisis challenged Franciscans to reclaim their identity and mission, the story of Francis was retold in the community in order to understand how the charism of Francis could be applied and appropriated in the new, contemporary context. In our own times the whole church again faces a major crisis: Christians of all denominations are returning to our traditions to claim resources that can help us redefine our identity as people of faith and our mission in the world. It is time once again to tell the story of Francis.

In every generation the stories of Francis have been used as "formation" documents to instruct and prepare new members of the order. These stories helped form new generations of Franciscans seeking to be faithful to their vocation in situations that were very different from those faced by Francis or the first friars. These narratives formed the cohesive center of the communities in which they were told. We believe that God is calling a new generation of Franciscans, one that transcends denominational lines in the church.

We chose to tell stories of Francis in the format of this book because we are convinced that stories can be more effective than doctrinal statements in communicating the truth. Stories and the images they evoke engage the life of a reader. As we read, we imaginatively enter into the landscape of a story. The meaning of the story is found not in doctrine to be understood by the head, but in images to be embraced by the heart.

1

A story is a powerful medium because it resembles the very nature of human experience. Our lives are meaningful to the degree to which we are able to weave all of our life experience into a story of some kind. A story with plot, characters, action, discourse, and location is the structure of human experience. Because of this, a story has the power to interpret human reality in profound ways. We tell the stories of Francis to initiate a conversation between each text and our own context, a dialogue between our story and the story of Francis. Thus in every chapter we provide what we call a personal cultural history exercise: a series of questions that can be used for journaling, reflection, and discussion that we hope will enable the reader to dig more fruitfully into the rich soil of his or her own culture. Similarly we provide social analysis reflections and exercises to deepen our understanding of how the Franciscan story can be creatively appropriated in our own socio-economic context.

What can be said about the stories of Francis can also be said about the scriptures included in each chapter: these too are stories that challenge us with images of a radical alternative. These stories have the ability to disturb as well as to animate and energize the reader. When a story is read, in a very real sense it is not the reader who interprets the story, but the story that interprets the reader. We may read a story from the world of Francis (or from the gospel!) and say, "How very strange." But when we return in our imagination to our own context, it may be our world and not that of Francis which seems strange. Through the medium of the story and the imagination of the reader, the past becomes present. We are invited to pick up the plot line with our lives and live out in our own context this open-ended story that stretches from century to century, from moment to moment.

The story of Francis not only interprets our contemporary reality, but also can empower us to construct reality in a distinctly Franciscan way. We are called not to imitate Francis or to agree to a doctrinal platform, but to become active participants in an open-ended story. Our participation in that story will require a fresh and creative appropriation of it in new and ever-changing circumstances. We can only do what we can imagine, and the stories of Francis enable us to imagine new ways of living out the gospel of Jesus Christ.

We acknowledge our indebtedness to the Franciscan community for preserving and retelling the story of Francis down through the ages. Thomas of Celano, an early contemporary of Francis, will be cited as a major source, as will Bonaventure, who wrote his version of the Francis story some forty years after the death of Francis. We also wish to acknowledge two Franciscans whose more contemporary interpretations have greatly influenced our thinking. These are Eloi Leclerc, the European author of *The Canticle of Creatures: Symbols of Union*, and Leonardo Boff, the Brazilian author of *Saint Francis, A Model for Human Liberation*.

A reader interested in learning more about the life of St. Francis might want to read one or more of his biographies. Of particular interest are *Saint Francis of Assisi* by Thomas of Celano and *Saint Francis, A Model for Human Liberation* by Leonardo Boff.

Process of the Book

The method of this book assumes that a number of elements working together in a flowing, interactive, and dynamic fashion are essential to long-lasting social transformation grounded in biblical faith. These elements include theological reflection, scriptural study, social analysis, reflection on personal history and experience, and active response. Each element depends upon the others for its full meaning. Every chapter in the book is composed of these elements and of a specific Franciscan narrative around which the aforementioned elements revolve. In this way we have sought to ground this inquiry into contemporary discipleship in the "circle of praxis," an ongoing process of reflection on social reality and action that aims to transform that reality. This term was first used by liberation theologians to describe a recurring cycle involving experience, social analysis, planning, and action.

In this introductory discussion of narrative we have mentioned at the elements of scripture study, theological reflection, personal cultural history, and Franciscan narrative. A few words might be useful regarding the remaining two elements, social analysis and action response.

Social analysis ("signs of our times"): We have said that we best imitate Francis by following Jesus in a creative and fresh appropriation of the story of Francis for our own context. Our context is infinitely complex, changing with tremendous speed, and, of course, multifaceted. It is political, economic, social, local, international, psychological, environmental, and spiritual. Some would say that the particular circumstances of our day constitute a *kairos* moment, a moment pregnant with crisis, opportunity, and a call to discipleship. In order to appropriate we must dig into and seek to understand this complex contemporary context. We must not shy away — as so many of us are prone to do — from the quest to unravel the seemingly overwhelming social realities of our day. Without so doing, we cannot creatively appropriate the gospel story.

Action response (invitation to respond): It is far too easy and too common to avoid allowing our newly gained insight to change the way in which we live. The action response component is meant to challenge us to live a deeper understanding of discipleship discovered in renewed reflection on the Franciscan tradition.

Finally, we hope and intend that this book be used primarily by people reflecting on it together with other people with whom they share a significant level of trust, caring, and accountability. This intent rests upon our belief that the community of believers is an essential part of Christian discipleship — and upon our own experiences, which have taught us that transformative learning happens best in the context of community.

A Few Comments on an Ecumenical Experiment

Across wide denominational lines, people of faith are recognizing with increasing clarity that we are in a global crisis that demands a new response from the church. It is not a time for clinging to our separateness as denominations; nor is this a time to abandon our traditions. We as Christians are being called to go more deeply into our common tradition to return to our roots. This is the meaning of "radical"—a going to the roots. To reclaim our tradition, our history, our story as gospel people is to be radical. To reclaim our roots is also to create a new basis for ecumenicity, a foundation for unity that is far greater than the historical differences that separate the different bodies of the church universal.

The authors of this volume hope that this is evident in the work to follow. We are very different—two Catholics, two Protestants; two men and two women; two ordained and two laity. And yet herein was the tremendous gift of our time together as we gathered for a period of months to reflect on the story of Francis, the gospel story, and our own stories.

Perhaps you can imagine some of the conversation at late-night or early-morning gatherings as the four of us wrestled with, for example, the idea of "sainthood" itself. Many in the Catholic community are all too familiar with the lives of the saints because they were exhorted to strive to imitate these examples of perfection. Saints were admirable, perhaps, but in no way imitable. The residue of such devotion to the saints was, for many Roman Catholics, a pervasive sense of guilt and failure. The Protestant community, we found, has a different problem. Eager to purify the church of what it saw to be the excesses of "hagiography," or what had become in the view of some the "worship of saints," Protestants rejected outright a rich tradition of individuals and communities in the history of the church. Yet this tradition of the saints, though predating the Reformation, is "protestant" in the deepest sense of the word: it embodies a prophetic alternative to the status quo that calls the church to reform.

For Protestant and Catholic alike, the lives of the saints can model liberating alternatives. This cloud of witnesses has the power to reform and transform the church by calling each of us to our own vocation of sainthood, to transformed lives. In the volume to follow, we have sought to place ourselves in dialogue with one of those saints, Francis of Assisi, to learn how he and his community responded creatively to the struggles faced in their own historical moment.

Our intent in these reflections is not really to call others to imitate Francis. In fact, we best imitate Francis by following Jesus in a creative appropriation of the gospel story for our own context. Francis' consuming goal was to follow Jesus. In hearing the story of how the saint of Assisi sought to live out a radical discipleship, we find new perspectives on how to live out our call to be followers of Jesus. Our hope is to inspire spiritual, political, and historical reflection and meditation on the life of Francis; to dialogue with his life and witness; and to reflect deeply on the questions that these raise. Jesus first introduced us to the ideas of Francis. But Francis can reintroduce us to Jesus in a radical way. This story is then offered to all, not just those in Franciscan or Catholic communities, but to all Christians in the universal church who are trying to follow Jesus at a time of historical crisis.

Prologue

WHY YOU, FRANCIS? WHY YOU?

One day when St. Francis was coming back from the woods, where he had been praying, and was at the edge of the forest, Brother Masseo went to meet him, as he wanted to find out how humble he was, and he said to St. Francis, half jokingly: "Why after you? Why after you? Why after you?"

St. Francis replied: "What do you mean, Brother Masseo?" "I mean, why does all the world seem to be running after you, and everyone seems to want to see you and hear you and obey you? You are not a handsome man. You do not have great learning or wisdom. You are not a nobleman. So why is all the world running after you?" (Brown, 62–63).

After Jesus himself, Francis of Assisi stands as the most popular and best-known figure in Christian history. Despite this, or perhaps because of it, we choose to add yet another volume to the already abundant material about him. Why?

Two inextricably related reasons motivate us. First, we are convinced that the saint of Assisi has a crucial message for us: for today's non-poor, the privileged of the world, the affluent of the late twentieth century.

We address this book primarily to the non-poor who wish to understand the meaning of Christian commitment in an increasingly impoverished world. Modern life suffers from, and paradoxically foments, isolation, injustice, violence, greed, and alienation from friendship and community. We believe that the values and spirituality of Francis contain a great lesson for contemporary U.S. society. Our offering, then, is an exploration of

7

the outrageousness of the Poverello who found joy and fulfill-ment in walking at the margins of acceptable society.

Yet his message, surprisingly, does not condemn us; rather, it invites us to walk a similar journey—a pathway which moves toward the New Creation (see Isa. 65:17–25). Moreover, despite our geographical, historical, psychological, and even spiritual distance from him, Francis' message contains a relevance and modernity to which his enduring popularity gives testimony. His message, calling to us from the past, points to the joy, the pain, and, yes, the hilarity of constant conversion. We believe that Francis' spirituality embodies a convergence of mysticism, lib-eration theology, and prophetic evangelism that speak loudly to those contemporary Christians who long to do something about inequity and poverty, about consuming consumerism and driven emptiness.

The second reason for this book complements the first: it can be described as Francis' discomfort factor. Like it or not, the life of this popular Christian saint presents us with startling paradoxes. An enormously free and spontaneous person, he nev-ertheless adhered faithfully to the institutional church; a fully alive human being, he embraced suffering; a true lover, he chose celibacy; born into relative affluence, he practiced a literal pov-erty. These and so many other aspects of Francis' life inevitably give us pause to ponder today: that is, unless we have the ques-tionable ability to ignore these unsettling aspects of his person-ality and deal only with the sentimental and "popular" sides of this complex man—his joy, love for nature, and familiarity with animals. As honest persons we need to delve into the real, flesh and blood, historical Francis. Otherwise we risk missing some-thing of the essence underlying his more familiar traits. There-fore we attempt here to present Francis to first-world readers in as complete a fashion as possible.

Both of these reasons for yet another book about Francis of Assisi require at least a brief look at his life in its historical framework. It is impossible to understand this person—as it is impossible to understand any human being—without at least a rudimentary grasp of the world that he inhabited.

The end of the twelfth and beginning of the thirteenth centuries, when Francis lived, have been described as a time of awakening in Europe. The so-called Dark Ages had given way to the Middle Ages. The next hundred years would witness the beginning of the Renaissance, the rebirth of culture and the real beginning of modern times. Among the many signs that this awakening was taking place was that Western Europe was becoming an area of surplus population, surplus productivity, and accelerated economic development. In addition, or as a consequence, the breakdown of the feudal system was leading to the emergence of city-states and a middle class. Feudalism would last a couple more centuries but the seeds of its destruction had been sown, and this, together with rising affluence, constitutes the central historical reality in the life of St. Francis.

Where wealth abounds can poverty be absent? The underside of new economic realities was a growing impoverishment of the masses. For in this incipient capitalistic system, as in its more sophisticated expressions, some people gained while most suffered. Francis saw this phenomenon and reacted to it vigorously.

The Catholic church at that time was at the height of its power and influence. This was not an unmitigated good. Not two hundred years later—a very short time in the 2,000-year history of the Roman communion—Pope Alexander VI would epitomize the corruption that overtook the church. And three hundred years after Francis the Protestant Reformation swept across Europe.

Within this historical and geographical reality, one can capsulize Francis' life with relative ease. Born in 1182, he was the son of a very successful cloth merchant, Pietro Bernardone, and a French woman, Lady Pica. At age twenty, after a comfortable and somewhat frivolous youth at the head of a group called "Merrymakers," the future saint marched off to one of the numerous wars then being fought between Italy's city-states. Imprisonment, sickness, and consequent disillusionment followed quickly, and Francis began to sense a different call. In dreams he heard himself called to another kind of chivalry—that of following "the great King." Tired of military adventurism, the young Francis began to divest himself of his considerable material possessions, thereby incurring his father's displeasure. A life-changing break with Don Pietro came in front of Assisi's good bishop when Francis literally removed the clothes given him by his father and uttered the startling statement: "From now on, I can walk naked before the Lord, no longer saying 'my father, Pietro Bernardone,' but 'Our Father who art in Heaven.'"

Thenceforth Francis followed Jesus according to his understanding of what that meant. First, he thought that the call he heard to "rebuild my church" referred to broken-down chapels around Assisi. The youth collected stones and other materials to refurbish these buildings. Gradually, as others joined him, he came to realize that his was a deeper and further-reaching vocation. The growing brotherhood (and, thanks to Clare, the sisterhood) helped Francis see that God had chosen him to inspire a great movement of renewal in the church. The rest of his life was lived following that ideal.

Some highlights of the years following Francis' dramatic conversion include his vision and nurturing of community, his mission of peace to the Sultan, and his deep friendships, especially with Clare. These and other events in Francis' life point to years of intense activity combined with an all-abiding sense of God's presence.

Francis was by all accounts passionate, impulsive, extroverted, fun-loving, and poetic. He may well also have been moody, given to introspection, mystical, demanding, and at times fearful. He was Italian, after all, possessed of the substantial gifts as well as the wonderful paradoxes of that singular people.

During the final period of his life Francis wrote the Canticle of Creation, perhaps the best known of his recorded words. It summed up the saint's abiding and integrating sense of God and God's presence in all that exists. Two years before his death Francis received the wounds of the Crucified in his hands, feet, and side. This gift of God sealed his closeness to the Savior and prepared him for his final days on earth. These were marked by great suffering as well as enormous joy. Francis of Assisi died on October 3, 1226 at age forty-four.

This "distant mirror" held up to our times and our struggles leads us to confront the contradictions we face in our world today, but with a hope born of grace alone. For Francis offers us the possibility of true joy, freedom, and love extending far beyond the boundaries of the familiar and based on an experience of God's mercy. Francis challenges us, not by avoiding human suffering and the negative side of human existence, but by embracing them.

Thus in coming to know Francis as we wrote this book, we increasingly encountered him as a prime example of God's Fool. From the moment he got down from his horse and forced himself to embrace a leper at the beginning of his conversion, Francis saw the world in all its glorious absurdity—and acted on what he saw. He stood naked before his father and fellow Assisians in the bishop's courtyard; he sang to the birds; he lived the rest of his life at the margins of society. The biblical and theological notion of "the Fool" has thus enlivened these pages and is, perhaps, the one great lesson we, the authors, take from this labor. We shall return to it throughout the book and in our epilogue.

Finally, this walk with Francis, at a distance of eight centuries, is placed at the disposal of Christians in the First World. We offer it to all who are troubled by the poverty of affluence, by the insults to God's creation, by demeaning human misery all around. We offer it to an ecumenical community that seeks to link faith with action as global citizens. To you, dear brothers and sisters, members of the household of faith in Jesus the Christ, we offer this modest attempt, as we strive together to move beyond the limitations imposed by fear, attachment to possessions, and weakness in our faith. Our patron in this common, enduring enterprise is the subject of this book, St. Francis of Assisi.

THE CONVERSION OF FRANCIS

Encounter with the Poor

And, raising his eyes toward his disciples, he said:
Blessed are you who are poor; for the kingdom of
    God is yours.
Blessed are you who are now hungry; for you will be
    satisfied.
Blessed are you who are now weeping; for you will
    laugh.
Blessed are you when people hate you, and when
    they exclude and insult you . . .
Rejoice and leap for joy on that day!
Behold, your reward will be great in heaven. For their
    ancestors treated the prophets in the same way.
                (Luke 6:20–23)

FRANCIS' STORY

All biographies of St. Francis point to his embrace of the leper on the Umbrian plain as the crucial moment in his initial conversion. Francis' encounter with the leper occurred very early—before his break with his father. Its impact on his life was unexpected and incalculable and, in many ways, set the tone for the rest of his life and mission, as well as for the lives and mission of his followers. Leonardo Boff writes about the "privilege of the poor in the conversion process of Francis" (Boff,

68). It is through the marginal, the lepers, the poor, that the Spirit led Francis into the mystery of the cross. And it is this encounter with the Crucified One that deepened Francis' vision of others on the cross.

According to the biographer Johannes Jörgensen, lepers occupied a special place among the sick and the poor during the Middle Ages. They were, in fact, looked upon as an image of the Redeemer himself, and were therefore the object of pious ministry. In the thirteenth century there were perhaps 19,000 homes for the care of lepers, one of which, near Assisi, was frequently passed by the young Francis. Yet, in spite of the care they were given, lepers were repulsed by the rest of society; they were severely restricted by laws that isolated them from all but the religiously motivated caretakers. Jörgensen (in *St. Francis of Assisi*) writes of Francis' reaction:

The [leper] hospital lay midway between Assisi and Portiuncula ... On his walks in this place, Francis now and then passed by the hospital, but the mere sight of it had filled him with horror. He would not even give alms to a leper unless someone else would take it for him. Especially when the wind blew from the hospital, and the weak, nauseating odor, peculiar to the leper, came across the road, he would hurry past with averted face and fingers in his nostrils.

It was in this that he felt his greatest weakness, and in it he was to win his greatest victory.

For one day, as he was as usual calling upon God, it happened that the answer came. And the answer was this: "Francis! Everything which you have loved and desired in the flesh, it is your duty to despise and hate, if you wish to know my will. And when you have begun thus, all that which now seems to you sweet and lovely will become intolerable and bitter, but all which you used to avoid will turn itself to great sweetness and exceeding joy."

These were the words which ... showed him the way he was to follow. He certainly pondered over these words in his lonely rides over the Umbrian plain and, just as he one day woke out of a reverie, he found the horse making a sudden movement, and saw on the road before him, only a few steps distant, a leper, in his familiar uniform.

Francis started, and even his horse shared in the movement, and his first impulse was to turn and flee as fast as he could. But there were the words he had heard within himself, so clearly before him — "what you used to abhor shall be to you joy and sweetness." . . . And what had he hated more than the lepers? Here was the time to take the Lord at His word — to show his good will . . . And with a mighty victory over himself, Francis sprang from his horse, approached the leper, from whose deformed countenance the awful odor of corruption issued forth, placed his alms in the outstretched wasted hand — bent down quickly and kissed the fingers of the sick man, covered with the awful disease, whilst his system was nauseated with the action . . .

When he again sat upon his horse, he hardly knew how he had got there. He was overcome by excitement, his heart beat, he knew not whither he rode. But the Lord had kept his word. Sweetness, happiness, and joy streamed into his soul — flowed and kept flowing, although his soul seemed full and more full — like the clear stream which, filling an earthen vessel, keeps on pouring and flows over its rim, with an ever clearer, purer stream . . .

The next day, Francis voluntarily wandered down the road he had hitherto always avoided . . . And when he reached the gate [to the leprosarium], he knocked, and when it was opened to him he entered. From all the cells the sick came swarming out — came with their half-destroyed faces, blind inflamed eyes, with club feet, with swollen, corrupted arms and fingerless hands. And all this dreadful crowd gathered around the young merchant, and the odor from their unclean swellings was so strong that Francis against his will for a moment had to hold his breath to save himself from sickness. But he soon recovered control of himself, he drew out the well-filled purse he had brought with him, and began to deal out his alms. And on every one of the dreadful hands that were

*reached out to take his gifts he imprinted a kiss, as he had
done the day before.* (Jörgensen, 38-39)

As a result of this experience of coming close to the most
despised, Francis was filled with wonder and joy. Jesus' beatitudes (Luke 6:20–23) must have been very much on his mind
in this regard. "Blessed are you poor, yours is the kingdom of
heaven." The significance of this scripture, which had been in
the collective Christian memory since the time of Jesus, began
to emerge, enfleshed and vibrant, for Francis.

Thereafter he sought contact at the margins time and time
again, gradually allowing his own process of conversion to be
informed by the experience of encounter with the poor. At first
he had despised the thought of touching the abhorred leper, but
now the invitation to reconciliation was irresistible. Francis'
deeply entrenched habit of pushing the leper to the edges of his
space, as far away from him physically and emotionally as possible, was forever broken.

For Francis the order of things was turned upside down, just
as it had been for the apostles, whose experience of Jesus so
often drew them into the mystery of the cross. Jesus, whom they
followed and called friend, embraced, mingled with, touched,
loved, cured, and broke bread with the outcasts, the marginal,
the unclean of his day. The lives of the poor or rejected ones
were and are intrinsically bound up with the journey of Jesus.
"Blessed are you poor," indeed! Consistently and deliberately
chosen encounters on the periphery of accepted society were
woven into the fabric of who Jesus became. In a social structure
shaped by exclusion of the leprous, the ritually unclean, the
"non-chosen," the women, the possessed, tax collectors, sinners—Jesus embraced them all, both individually and as social
groups. In fact, Jesus' very identity was as one who proclaimed
the good news to the poor; who announced the inbreaking of
the Reign of God; and who lived the announcement by being at
the side of the poor himself.

Encounter with Jesus in the Poor

In Francis' new upside-down order, his encounter with the
leper was indeed an encounter with this Jesus in the poor. The

story of the leper symbolizes Francis' journey across a tremendous psychological and emotional barrier. Once he was able to transcend that dreaded barrier, he seemed to be able to move beyond and allow himself to be open to the "other" whom he had previously imagined to be so awful. It allowed him to move forward in leaps and bounds on his own journey, and to surmount the barriers that separate the clean from the unclean, the desirable from the undesirable, the haves from the have-nots. Once he was given the grace to do that, everything was changed for him. As Francis embraced a vivid example of human misery, he tasted great joy; the sweetness he experienced revealed God's presence pervading his meeting with the outcast. "Sweetness," the very word Francis had used earlier to describe his own profoundly ecstatic experience of God, is now used by him to describe the experience of knowing a leper.

In *A Theology of Liberation*, Gustavo Gutiérrez writes about the evolution of our encounters with God. Moving from the mountain top to the ark of the covenant to the temple to the neighbor, the Jewish and Christian traditions have called us to celebrate the sacrament of the "other," especially the most marginal, as blessed location of the indwelling Spirit. "God's temple is human history; the 'sacred' transcends the narrow limits of the places of worship. We find the Lord in our encounters with [others], especially the poor, marginated, and exploited ones. An act of love towards them is an act of love toward God. This is why Yves Congar speaks of the 'sacrament of our neighbor,' who as a visible reality reveals to us and allows us to welcome the Lord" (Gutiérrez, 115).

"Blessed Are You Who Weep Now . . . "

Encountering the impoverished, walking for a while in the world of the marginalized, and being with the have-nots of our world is a necessary step on the discipleship journey. Our vision thereafter is shaped by this encounter. We realize, and never forget, the privileged perspective of the poor who see reality with a clarity of vision that we may never achieve. Our souls are touched by the encounter as well, and a blessed sorrow over the pain and injustice of impoverishment and marginalization fills the crevices of our being. The painful side of the paradox—the misery of poverty—presents itself once again.

> Look, O Lord, upon my distress:
>   all within me is in ferment . . .
> Give heed to my groaning;
>   there is no one to console me.
>   (Lam. 1:20–21)

Deep mourning over the condition of the poor may be the first step we non-poor can take to internalize the beatitudes: "Blessed are you who are now weeping; you shall laugh." Mourning implies a terrible sense of loss, of regret, an acknowledgment of the real, and a feeling of pain in the face of that reality. Weeping and mourning emerge from our affective side and are profoundly healthy emotions for those of us who are more privileged—who will never fully share the lot of the poor, but who at least can weep over the tragedy of human suffering. Emotions help describe us as whole people and, if joined with righteous indignation at the injustices that cause the leprosies of our world, can lead us toward a relinquishment of the power and privilege that maintain injustice, and toward a solidarity with the poor in their claim on justice.

The grief-stricken wailing of Lamentations was written in the days of the prophet Jeremiah, the sixth century B.C.E., a turning point in the story of the people of Israel, and an unprecedented time of crisis for a people who failed to hear the prophetic call to social transformation. The temple was destroyed and its ritual interrupted; leading citizens were taken into exile; and the disintegration of society resulted in captivity which separated the people from the land that carried their communal identity.

Our times, too, are times of crisis. Our society faces escalating social and moral disintegration, a devastating captivity to ways of life that perpetrate injustice, marginalization, and extreme poverties of body and soul. The prophetic call of Jeremiah echoes around us and we, too, are wont to ignore it. Exile seems inevitable, and its parameters are beginning to emerge: massive indebtedness (both public and private); increasing poverty; lack of meaningful work; rampant violence (in structures, streets, and even our homes); isolation from community; a loss of roots; vast emptiness in place of meaningful existence; and so on.

The book of Lamentations moves from confession of sin through profound grief to strong faith in the constancy of Yahweh's love and fidelity. We, too, can move from confession of sin and deep mourning through righteous anger toward a hope-filled embrace of a better, more life-giving Way.

The Paradox of Joy

In the context of our mourning, however, the joy described by Francis in his encounter with the leper presents us with a disturbing paradox. In itself, contact with poor people does not generate the sort of sweetness that Francis claims—at least not at first. Even for Francis the leper initially caused "disgust and horror." Dehumanizing poverty and marginalization are ugly blights upon the contours of creation. Our encounter with those who are crucified and who are struggling for liberation brings us, as it brought Francis, face to face with excruciating pain and offers much food for reflection. Indeed, to walk with the poor, to share their lives and struggles, to accompany the "least" of our brothers and sisters in the painful places they inhabit can and must occasion anger, rage, and the desire to change the way things are. Paradoxically, this encounter with those suffering on the margins can also occasion amazing joy. The claim of the gospel ("Yours is the reign of God . . . You shall laugh!") and of St. Francis that one can find God and profound pleasures of the soul in meeting the poor is hard to believe, especially for the non-poor.

Initially, perhaps, we can only accept this on faith, but slowly we will experience it, sometimes in contrast with the barrenness of affluence, as we summon the courage, not to make poverty look better, but to step into the suffering of the poor ones as

Francis did. There, in the place of empty consumerism, it is possible to encounter life-giving values. In the place of individualism we can find common struggle; in the place of greed we frequently see generosity beyond belief. Here we do have a paradox. Poverty is ugly and dehumanizing; it is an evil that must be eliminated. Yet, in encountering the poor, we often discover beauty and graced humanity. Indeed, in encountering the poor ones of our world, we find God.

Accompaniment: A Dialogue of the Heart

Each of us, no doubt, can recall moments of grace-filled interaction that have called us beyond what we are toward what we can be, both as individuals and as communities of faith. For many in recent years, these moments of grace have taken place in encounters like that of Francis with the leper. Profound conversion, and the resultant freedom of the spirit and deep joy, have so often begun in a dialogue of the heart with the poor ones — a dialogue of the heart, the mind, and the soul that has shaped forever the intent and the direction of our lives.

The dialogue might take place in our own communities — with the homeless or refugees, with those who are impoverished or sick with AIDS. It might take us to Appalachia or the inner city, to family farms in the heartland or the Rio Grande, to Africa, Haiti, or Latin America.

A few years ago, during the worst of the war in El Salvador, just such a dialogue took place at the tomb of martyred archbishop Oscar Romero. Some of us U.S. citizens present heard the stories of a people just then shelled and bombed and burned out of their homes, displaced from their lands by a military operation called Phoenix. The Salvadorans had come to the cathedral, which was still unfinished, bleak, and raw, in solidarity with those whose daily lives were war-torn, bleak, and raw. They had come to the cathedral — that protected, public, blessed place — to make a human appeal and a political statement, risking all in their search for freedom from war. The cathedral, that skeletal monument to the poverty of a people, shored up their courage to speak.

The dialogue that day was about human suffering and reconciliation. The Salvadorans knew well that the bombs came
from U.S. factories; that support for the war being waged against
them came at the rate of $1.5 million a day from our country.
We each said, *"Lo siento mucho,"* an inadequate gesture, "I'm
sorry" ... a concrete attempt to express the pain, remorse, and
embarrassment we felt. Individually and as a people — and in the
name of a people — that day at the tomb of Romero, we were
embraced and forgiven.

Later that year the dialogue continued. Tired of living
dependent lives in refugee camps, the people had decided to go
home. It was time to return to cultivate their land, to reclaim
their roots, to enflesh values of life in the midst of death and
violence, and we U.S. citizens, the forgiven ones, were invited
to accompany them: to walk for a while side by side, to step in
each other's footprints, to search together for solutions, to celebrate together, and to cry together.

On the way to the *campo* we laughed together and prayed
together, we held the children together, hauled debris from the
bombed-out shells of the village together, and broke bread in
Eucharist together. We stood together when the army came, and
we wept as the soldiers separated us.

It was the sort of time when dialogue could lead to an understanding of the spirit of a people — a time to hear another's
language and see another's culture in a new way and to understand better the hopes and fears of these most impoverished
ones. What we learned dramatically turned our non-poor perceptions of the world upside down, as the encounter with the
leper turned Francis' world upside down: "Blessed are the
poor."

The Role of the Non-Poor

Francis' embrace of the leper was both a personal leap of
faith and, at the same time, a social statement akin to the sort
of social statements that paved Jesus' way to the cross. What
social statements are we called to make in the face of the pov-

erties of our own world? In other words, what is the role of the non-poor in relation to the liberation journeys of those who are impoverished and marginalized, not only in Latin America, but also in our own country and in other parts of the world? How do we respond to the fear and rage we often feel when faced with poverty? How do we respond to the grace and goodness we encounter? How do we learn to move from pity to love, from charity to justice, from the one poor one to the many? How do we discern the causes of poverty and identify ways to challenge and overcome exploitative structures? What is our responsibility in the creation of a more just and peaceful world?

Our response might best be summed up by the word "accompaniment": to deviate from other pathways for a while (and then forever), to walk with those on the margins, to be with them, to let go. Accompaniment is an idea so radical and difficult for us to comprehend that its power and significance reveal themselves to our Western and Northern minds only slowly and with great difficulty. Through this encounter with Christ at the margins, we, who with Francis once saw the poor only as the "other," the feared one, the object of dread, then pity, then charity, can, as individuals and societies, experience a profound, ongoing, Spirit-led conversion of heart, soul, and mind. Slowly our centers of gravity move outside of ourselves and we find ourselves suddenly dancing with the Poverello and his despised friends in unknown places and with great joy.

It is a way of life well known to Francis — and to the Oscar Romeros and Ita Fords* among us, who probed the depths of incarnation, crucifixion, and resurrection, and who knew that their souls would never be the same. It is a way of life that makes sense out of Jesus' embrace of and friendship with the outcast.

It is an idea that at first glimpse seems utterly simple but,

---

*Oscar Romero, martyred bishop of El Salvador, and Ita Ford, one of four U.S. churchwomen martyred in El Salvador in 1980, both expressed and lived their desire simply to walk with the suffering poor of that land.

when tried, stretches the limits of our theological understanding and our spirituality, challenges our worldview, pushes us toward horizons we never thought we could reach, and turns upside-down the question of our role in the creation of a more just and peaceful world.

Consider again the Sermon on the Mount:

> Blessed are you poor; yours is the Reign of God.
> Blessed are you who are hungry now; you shall be satisfied.
> Blessed are you who weep now; you shall laugh.
> Blessed are you when people hate you, drive you out, abuse you . . . your reward will be great.

Do we dare to believe it? Do we dare to believe that the poor and hungry will be satisfied and that the weeping will laugh? Do we dare to believe that in these times God incarnate is suffering crucifixion and redeeming us still? Witness the faith of so many who are poor! See how often they love one another back to life—see how they struggle together to bring about the Reign of God, the New Creation, beginning with the basic necessities of life—potable water, education, health care, and so forth. Can we allow the grace of their challenging embrace to permeate our lives?

The invitation to accompaniment is a fragile invitation into the heart of our Christian faith—an invitation to witness the Spirit present in the suffering and fidelity of the poor today. At some times the invitation is to an individual—a "stranger" inserted into the reality of a marginal world. In other situations, as in El Salvador, Haiti, and South Africa, the invitation has been extended to the international community in general to experience concretely the painful results of injustice and poverty. This welcoming is a real and specific gesture of reconciliation. In the world today, the lives of marginalized people in El Salvador, Guatemala, the Middle East, Bolivia, Peru, the Philippines, Korea, South Africa, and the cities and rural areas of our own country as well, are inextricably linked to our own—

too often through our systems and structures, even our values, that oppress them.

It is incredible, therefore, that we are even occasionally invited into their embrace as they seek a more humane existence. It is a remarkable opportunity—a gift of great courage from the poor of this world to the non-poor.

We are invited to move step by step from our positions of privilege into greater solidarity with the poor and with Christ who is incarnate on the margins of society. But our lifetime journey as non-poor must move beyond solidarity with the struggles of the marginalized, for the non-poor, too, are children of God, called to be subjects of our own stories. As a class, we also are necessary participants in the unique New Creation tasks given to us. As we accompany marginalized people—the poor ones or "lepers" of our world today—physically or politically, we begin to experience the truth that we are also embraced and accompanied by them. As we struggle to find God in their land (the hovels and barrios, favelas and tenements so alien to many of us), as we struggle for the liberation of our cultural soul (so often captive to consumerism, to the media, to Madison Avenue, to the rat race of superficial living), we learn that they are the Beloveds of this world who are drinking from the Cup of the One Who Accompanied us all. Their suffering and their efforts to claim a more human existence are one with the suffering of Jesus and with his announcement of the inbreaking Reign of God. The lives of these marginal ones continue the crucifixion and promise resurrection. As a redemptive presence in our broken world, the poor accompany us.

Gift to the Non-Poor

As we are accompanied, everything changes. Common struggle begins to replace destructive individualism; generosity and concern for the other overcome individual and collective greed. Prayer, sacrament, community, and images of God are all transformed. Prayer becomes prophetic and, as Walter Brueggemann says, "impolite." Eucharist is nourishment for the long haul, a deep source of consolation and joy, and a profound challenge always to share the bread of hunger. Reconciliation is deep and gratifying, grounded in the most painful memories born from a dialogue of the heart—a dialogue about poverty and human suffering, about isolation, neglect, and violence—but clearly a dialogue leading toward new ways of being brother and sister in a broken world. Community—peoples in solidarity on their journey/our journey to liberation—becomes an essential element of life, a supportive, challenging, and life-giving element. Images of God are profoundly incarnational, drawn from this encounter with suffering, struggling humanity.

Francis' moment with the leper, then, has become a paradigm for understanding Francis. It was a grace-filled moment for him, a time of crisis, a *kairos*. We reflect on it because it explains so much about him. Francis always pointed to lepers and to the "dwelling places of lepers" as places where Franciscans should be. Francis' encounter with the leper was a moment of self-definition, self-revelation, and conversion. Our encounter at the margins of society can be a means of understanding ourselves as well—a grace-filled *kairos* for us as individuals and as a society.

OUR STORIES

Reflect on your own relationship to people who are poor or marginalized. Go back into your memory and recall your earliest conscious experience with people you considered poor or outcast. If you were poor as a child, recall when you first realized it. In either case:

• What did you think? What did you feel? What did you do?

• How did the experience influence your subsequent impressions of poor people?

• What are the images, characteristics, and assumptions about poor people that you absorbed as you grew up?

• Imagine someone poor visiting your home. How would you feel? Imagine someone who has much more money, social status, or education than you have visiting your home. How would you feel?

SIGNS OF OUR TIMES

We know that today the leper is not only a single individual whom we might encounter as we go out from familiar to new realities. Today the leper is the thousands of homeless who huddle in subway stations or on steam grates in our cities. The leper is the numberless battered women who seek shelter from impossible domestic situations. The leper is the deinstitutionalized mental patient walking the streets in a daze. The leper is the "third world" hungry—one *billion* of them—who could be fed with the excess of our tables. The leper is the children of impoverished countries who will never have quality of life because of preventable diseases, poor education, and overcrowded job markets. The leper is the women of the Southern Hemisphere, old before their time from bearing too many children as insurance against destitution in their declining years.

The lepers of today, tragically, are the majority of the earth's five billion people, the two-thirds of humanity who live in poverty and the countless others who are continually pushed to the periphery of our societies. In our own time we have unprecedented access to information about the breadth and depth of "leprosy" in the human condition. With modern communications technologies, we cannot *not* know that three million men, women, and children in the United States and 100 million around the world are homeless; that one-fifth of the children in the United States live below the poverty line; that 880 million adults in the world are illiterate; that 60 percent of the people in the world live in countries where the annual per capita income is below $2000.

Americans [in the U.S.] spend $5 billion each year on special diets to lower their calorie consumption, while the world's poorest 400 million people are so undernourished they are likely to suffer stunted growth, mental retardation, or death. As water from a single spring in France is bottled and shipped to the prosperous around the world, 1.9 billion people drink and bathe in water contaminated with deadly parasites and pathogens, and more than half of humanity lacks sanitary toilets.

Those at the very bottom of the economic ladder form a distinct subclass. Defined as those who spend 80 percent of their income on food but still lack sufficient calories to meet their metabolic needs, this undernourished class accounts for perhaps one-third of the absolute poor, or 400 million people. (*Worldwatch Paper* 92, 5, 21)

According to Joe Holland and Peter Henriot, S.J., in their classic book *Social Analysis: Linking Faith and Justice*, "social analysis can be defined as the effort to obtain a more complete picture of a social situation by exploring its historical and structural relationships." Some questions to ponder in the light of the "signs of the times" described above:

What kinds of decisions have led to this global situation? Who has made and continues to make these decisions? Who has benefitted from these decisions? Who bears the burden? Who can make decisions that could change the situation? How can you participate in this change?

INVITATION TO RESPOND

Having read of Francis' encounter with the leper and reflected on it in light of the beatitudes, we are called to respond with action. Like Jesus and Francis, we are commanded by God to "bring good news to the poor," and we are assured by the life of Jesus and the witness of Francis that we will find good news among the poor. But to do both, we must move to the margins where we can encounter the poor.

Draw a circle that defines your "familiar world." Write in it all those whose lives regularly intersect with your own. Write outside your circle those whose lives rarely touch yours. Begin with the following list, but add to it from your own experience.

immediate family
coworkers
neighbors
homeless people
refugees
people with AIDS
people of other racial groups than your own
people who are poor
those in prison
people with physical disabilities
the elderly
the mentally or emotionally ill

Note that in his encounter with the leper Francis had to go out. He did not come upon the leper until he had moved toward him, however unconsciously or unknowingly.

Have you felt a call to go out of your familiar world toward the "other," the stranger, the needy one? Think of a particular instance when you have experienced such an invitation. Have you allowed yourself to accept? If not, what held you back?

Upon seeing the leper, Francis got down from his horse in order to embrace him. This was a further act of going out. Have you allowed yourself, even forced yourself literally to move to another place in order to embrace a hurting world, to walk in the shoes of a suffering person, to understand the poor? How?

Let God lead you again and again to the "leper," whoever he or she might be. Let the experience be a reflective one, not a dutiful going among the poor, but a conscious and meditative move out from the familiar to the world of hurt—perhaps in the very same soup kitchen or hospice that you have visited before. Allow the experience to challenge your assumptions about the margins and to push you toward appropriate response.

2

FRANCIS AND RELINQUISHMENT

Ongoing Conversion

As he was setting out on a journey, a man ran up, knelt down before him, and asked him, "Good teacher, what must I do to inherit eternal life?" ... "You know the commandments: 'You shall not kill; you shall not commit adultery; you shall not steal; you shall not bear false witness; you shall not defraud; honor your father and your mother.'"

He ... said to him, "Teacher, all of these I have observed from my youth." Jesus, looking at him, loved him and said to him, "You are lacking in one thing. Go, sell what you have, and give to [the] poor and you will have treasure in heaven; then come, follow me." At that statement his face fell, and he went away sad, for he had many possessions. Jesus looked around and said to his disciples, "How hard it is for those who have wealth to enter the kingdom of God!" The disciples were amazed at his words. (Mark 10:17–24)

FRANCIS' STORY

Here we look at the moment in the life of Francis when he stripped himself naked in the courtyard of the cathedral, in front of his own family, the bishop, and the townspeople of Assisi.

By this time, Francis had experienced the transforming

encounter with the leper. In chapter 1 we reflected on that story in which Francis is called to conversion in an encounter with the poor. Soon after that, Francis heard a voice telling him to "rebuild my church." He sold his father's goods and used the proceeds for the work of repairing a ruined chapel called San Damiano. Francis later went into hiding from his father but was found and imprisoned by the elder Bernardone. The conflict between father and son grew until it reached the breaking point described below. This was a decisive moment in Francis' conversion, when Francis took the leap of faith from his world into that of the poor through a radical relinquishment of status and security.

But when his father saw that he could not bring Francis back from the way he had undertaken, he was roused by all means to get his money back. The man of God [Francis] had desired to offer it and expend it to feed the poor and to repair the buildings of that place. But he [Francis] who had no love for money could not be misled by any aspect of good in it; and he who was not held back by any affection for it was in no way disturbed by its loss. Therefore, when the money was found, which he who hated the things of this world so greatly and desired the riches of heaven so much had thrown aside in the dust of the window sill, the fury of his raging father was extinguished a little, and the thirst of his avarice was somewhat allayed by the warmth of discovery. He then brought his son before the bishop of the city, so that, renouncing all his possessions into his father's hands, he [Francis] might give up everything he had. Francis not only did not refuse to do this, but he hastened with great joy to do what was demanded of him.

When he [Francis] was brought before the bishop, he would suffer no delay or hesitation in anything; indeed, he did not wait for any words nor did he speak any, but immediately putting off his clothes and casting them aside, he gave them back to his father. Moreover, not even retaining his trousers, he stripped himself completely naked before all. The bishop, however, sensing his disposition and admiring greatly his fervor and constancy, arose and drew him within his arms and covered him with the mantle he was wearing. He understood clearly that the counsel was of God, and he understood that the actions of the man of God [Francis] that he had personally witnessed contained a mystery. He immediately, therefore, became his helper and cherishing him [Francis] and encouraging him he embraced him in the bowels of charity. (Celano, VI, 16–17)

Young Francis had for some time been the topic of conversation around the hearths of Assisi undoubtedly. Some must have pitied him for what they saw to be the ravings of a madman. For others his "antics" were a source of amusement or scorn. There could be no doubt in anyone's mind that Francis had not been the same since he returned from war with a deadly fever. But all that had gone before would seem tame in comparison with this moment. How fast did word spread around town that there was some commotion down at the cathedral and that Francis was at the center of it? How quickly would the townspeople gather to witness this latest chapter in the ongoing scandal of the Bernardone family? What did they think when Francis dropped his cloak? What emotions did they feel when he stood naked before them all? Did anyone there in the courtyard, Francis included, really understand the significance of what they saw? Do we?

The story of Francis stripping himself naked in the bishop's courtyard conveys to us an essential moment in his conversion process. As Francis stood there naked, completely vulnerable before the bishop, his family, and the people of Assisi, he divested himself of much more than just his clothes and belongings. In effect he relinquished family identity and reputation and the security of his economic status. For Francis this moment was a literal and symbolic letting go of his former life.

But we misunderstand the significance of this moment if we think that it was for Francis an end in itself. Francis did not pursue poverty as an ascetic ideal of self-denial. For Francis this relinquishment was a practical means of relocating himself in relationship to the poor. His break from his former life and status in Assisi was the prelude to his life and work among the poor of the leper colony. Indeed, one cannot distinguish Francis' conversion experience from this journey toward the poor: they are one and the same. His encounter with the leper, selling of his father's goods, and stripping himself naked are all symbolic moments, steps in a conversion process. For Francis it is relationship to the poor which provides the genuine context for conversion.

In our own time, does relinquishment play an essential role in our own ongoing conversion as people of faith? This story from the biography of Francis has much to teach us, the non-poor, about the nature of our discipleship. But to understand Francis and the role of relinquishment in our own faith journey, we must look beyond Francis to the gospel upon which he based his life and witness. Several gospel texts became absolutely normative for the life and practice of the early Franciscan community. The text from Mark cited above is one of those. Our purpose here is to continue our dialogue with Francis about the creative ways in which he followed Jesus in his own place and time. Hearing this story of how Francis lived his radical discipleship, we gain new perspectives on how to live our call to follow Jesus. Now we delve more deeply into this gospel story to see from another perspective how this word can become flesh in our lives and in our place and time.

An Encounter "Along the Way"

A man ran up and knelt before him, and asked him, "Good teacher, what must I do to inherit eternal life?"

Immediately our story sets up an encounter between Jesus and an unnamed individual. The narrative begins to offer us clues about who this person is from the nature of their meeting. We notice that the man's approach to Jesus is formal and proper. He kneels before Jesus and calls him good teacher as a sign of respect. We suspect that this person has considerable social standing. The man asks about eternal life, a religious question that undoubtedly comes from the heart. Yet Jesus responds rather aloofly, "Why do you call me good?"

The Invitation to Discipleship

As if they were sparring with each other over the keeping of the ten commandments, Jesus deliberately inserts, "Do not defraud!" as a warning to the rich not to deprive workers of their just wage. Here the story takes a remarkable turn. Jesus looks upon the individual and loves him. Jesus' initial aloofness yields to a genuine love for the individual standing before him. Recognizing the potential for discipleship, Jesus issues to him an invitation:

> "You lack one thing; go, sell what you have, and give it to the poor, and you will have treasure in heaven; and come follow me."

At that, the sadness of the man betrays his inner struggle and, ultimately, his failure to respond to the invitation. As he turns away we learn for the first time that he was indeed a rich person, "for he had many possessions."

Placed side by side, the gospel text and the story of Francis are two analogous stories of "rich men" in a fundamental crisis that arises from the contradiction between the demands of discipleship and the possession of wealth in the presence of the poor. In response to this crisis, the one, genuinely seeking to move forward in his faith journey, is confronted by Jesus with this contradiction. Sadly, he turns away, unable to let go of his possessions and thus respond to the invitation. In the other story, the second rich man, from Assisi, takes a radical leap of faith; he relinquishes his hold on all worldly ties and possessions. Francis transposes himself from the world of his family and the emerging bourgeois class to the world of the most marginalized poor whose plight worsened as their numbers steadily increased.

We as "first-world" people may not think of ourselves as rich. Middle-class persons may not perceive themselves as well off or even financially secure, but if we look at the global reality, we know that we are indeed the rich, that the political and economic power wielded by the industrial Western nations makes us wealthy beyond comparison. In hearing this text, we as non-poor people of faith come to a crossroad in our own discipleship journey.

At this juncture it is important for us to reflect on what made it possible for one wealthy person, and apparently impossible for the other, to respond affirmatively to the invitation to discipleship.

The Gospel: A Scandal and Stumbling Block to the "First World"?

If we are honest with ourselves, the gospel story of the rich man is most disturbing. The "first-world" church's difficulty with this text is rooted in the recognition that Jesus' call to discipleship and man's inability to respond to that call challenge us directly. Non-poor people of faith have found this story very threatening because we have understood Jesus to mean that a contradiction exists between possessions and the demands of faith. Can we be who we are as middle-class people and still be faithful followers of Jesus? We must remember that Jesus looked upon the young man, loved him, and invited him to join his community. The non-poor are children of God and loved by Jesus. But when we open ourselves to this text, we are faced with the contradiction between authentic Christian faith and possessing more than we need while others lack the basic necessities of life.

The "first-world" church's difficulty with the encounter between Jesus and the rich man is not surprising. Even the discipleship community around Jesus struggled to come to grips with the radical nature of what Jesus was proposing. As we move to the second section of the text, we see that Jesus is openly skeptical about the ability of the rich to respond to the call of discipleship. To underscore this point, Jesus uses the metaphor of the camel and the eye of the needle, a bit of peasant humor that leaves no doubt about the conflict between wealth and discipleship. The disciples respond with astonishment, "Who then can be saved?" Our reaction as "first-world" Christians echoes that of the disciples themselves. Like them, the non-poor today have squirmed uncomfortably with this metaphor. We have softened its impact with interpretations that dilute the meaning of the story.

It is very difficult for "first-world" Christians, to "be with" this story for long without trying to find a theological loophole through which to escape. We have simply eliminated the contradiction by rewriting the gospel to suit ourselves. We have taken this challenging story and the hundreds of other scriptural passages that address economic justice and put them in a jar on the shelf.

The easiest way to resolve this dilemma has been to ignore it and to pretend that no contradiction is posed here. The contribution of Francis was to take the witness and words of the historical Jesus quite seriously and to strive to apply them radically to his own life. At the very least, we as people of faith must remain in dialogue with this gospel story even if it means being uncomfortable.

Continuing the dialogue, one might ask: What about us, the non-poor? Does this mean there is no place for us in the gospel story? The God of the poor does not reject us because we are non-poor or love us any less than the poor. Yet the oppression and impoverishment of our brothers and sisters demands a response from us. Christ beckons to us from the margins, in the human face of the poor, the "least of these," inviting each of us to join this struggle. If we, like Francis, are seeking to follow Jesus, we must begin to find ways to journey to the margins of society to encounter those on the "other side."

As we reflected in the previous chapter, the gospel calls us to the margins of society in order to bring about the conversion that is begun in our encounter with the poor. The conversion of Francis was a profound change from seeing the leper as an abhorrent and despised non-person to seeing him as a brother in whom Christ dwells. In Francis' conversion of heart, he began to feel and practice compassionate solidarity. In this chapter we reflect on the next stage of our response as we let go in order to enter more deeply into that conversion process. We are asked to move beyond our comfort zone, beyond the insulating boundaries of class and social status to places of greater risk, toward those on the margins.

As we are given the grace to encounter people on the other side of society from us, we quickly become aware of the tremendous abyss that exists between us and them. Beyond cultural differences, which should be celebrated but not obliterated, we begin to recognize that the abyss that separates us is rooted in racism, economic injustice, and fundamental social inequities. Our task as the non-poor is to remove the obstacles that we have created and that prevent the liberation of the poor and marginalized. Our task is to create the space needed by marginalized communities for their process of self-determination.

Our conversion may entail letting go of deeply held ways of seeing the world. As we emerge from the cocoon of middle-class existence and begin to see the world from the perspective of the poor, we discover a profoundly different reality. Our perspective is likely to be altered as we increasingly learn, with the help of the poor, to read reality from their perspective. Gradually we begin to understand our history and the forces that shape the present moment from the perspective of the "underside" of society. This is not only a profound shift in understanding but, on the basis of that new awareness, a conversion of the way in which we live.

Relinquishment is much more than giving up material goods. It means giving up prestige and privilege, learning to listen and to accept criticism and learning how to use our power differently and ultimately to share our power. At the very least, our task as the non-poor is to share the power available to us—our resources of wealth, education, influence, and access—with those who lack these things. This is not charity or "noblesse oblige." It is a fundamental letting go to allow the very structures that benefit us to be transformed so that they will no longer impede but will include and benefit others.

Our task as people of faith will be to refashion, indeed, to re-create more equitable, open, and inclusive systems and structures, not just in the religious community but in the larger society. At first it may seem that we are being asked to work against our own interests and to our disadvantage. As structures and systems yield to change, we may experience sharing power as a loss of power or even a taste of powerlessness. But ultimately, as conditions of justice, equality, and self-determination begin to take shape in concrete ways, we will understand that what we have been about is the transformation of power from the power of domination to the power of compassionate solidarity. New possibilities will emerge for reconciliation, friendship, and a genuine empowerment grounded in community.

In the end we are faced with the terrible paradox of Christian faith that defies human definitions of power. In the moment of the absolute powerlessness, indeed the complete self-abnegation of Jesus on the cross, God has radically overturned all human notions of power. Out of weakness comes strength; out of powerlessness comes power; out of death comes resurrection, life. This is part of the radical witness that Jesus, Paul, and Francis place before us: God's foolishness is wiser than human wisdom and God's weakness stronger than human strength.

Losing Ourselves, We Find Ourselves

The way of relinquishment is the lifelong process of removing the obstacles to loving and just relationships with our neighbors on this earth and of moving toward more genuine community among all of God's children, the kind of brotherhood and sisterhood envisioned by Francis. As we help to remove the obstacles to the liberation of others, we are simultaneously removing obstacles to our own liberation.

If we are ever to discover our true God-given identity, we must respond to this struggle for a just society and true community. We are called to a wholeness as human beings that is much greater than our identity as individuals. This wholeness cannot be fully discovered outside of justice in our society. What we are beginning to learn as non-poor people is that we, no less than the poor and marginalized, are dehumanized by the systems of oppression. The image of God in us—the image of our true humanity—is scarred because we have learned to coexist with the violence of injustice. Neither we nor the poor can be whole persons as long as injustice goes unchallenged. God's love for the poor is expressed in liberating and healing acts which show the people that God accompanies them. God's love for the non-poor is no less real. This love invites the non-poor to join God on the margins among the poor in order to find our true identity in relationship, in community, in the common struggle to transform the world.

Relinquishment and the Abundant Life

The call to relinquishment is grounded in the promise of abundant life and in the language of salvation. It is the essential gospel dialectic of losing one's life in order to find it. What we are asked to believe is a foolish proposition: the gospel promise that we will receive in return far more than what we give up.

> Peter began to say to [Jesus], "We have given up everything and followed you." Jesus said, "Amen, I say to you, there is no one who has given up house or brothers or sisters or mother or father or children or lands for my sake and for the sake of the gospel who will not receive a hundred times more now in this present age: houses and brothers and sisters and mothers and children and lands, with persecutions, and eternal life in the age to come." (Mark 10:28–31)

Jesus responds to Peter's need for some assurance that the decision to follow Jesus will not only entail the negative reality of "giving up." He promises that whatever has been relinquished for the gospel will be given back a hundred times more. He promises a harvest "in this present age," so bountiful as to boggle the mind of the peasant farmer.

Who among us can attempt the "negative" work of relinquishment without some positive vision that makes it worthwhile and even possible? How do we let go of many of the things in which we have come to find security, identity, and status, unless we nurture a hopeful, morally compelling vision of what is possible? Without this ability to imagine our society as a true community, or ourselves as transformed human beings, we will not be able to relax our grip on our socio-economic status quo.

Wendel Berry has said, "We are much more easily motivated by what we desire than by what we deplore." The essence of the prophetic task is to articulate a vision of the common good that has the power to capture the imagination of the people as a goal worthy of struggle and sacrifice. How can we begin to create a vision of our society which makes us willing to move out from behind the walls of our defenses into the unknown but hoped-for future and to stake our lives on such a foolish proposition as the Reign of God? For both Jesus and Francis, the vision of the Reign of God was that source of transforming power which animated and informed their sense of mission and community.

Let us now consider the response of the rich man / poor man from Assisi to the gospel call for relinquishment. Francis took the daring leap of faith from a position of privilege into the world of the poor. His renunciation of the world, though radical, was apparently not odious to him. We sense that for Francis the gospel promise was fulfilled, that what one receives in return is far more than what one has given up. Francis renounced the world only to have it given back with joy.

It was not long after his break with family and social life in Assisi that Francis was joined by others who formed with him a community among the poor. The story of Francis teaches us that the invitation and challenge to relinquishment is extended not just to individuals but to communities. We recall that the invitation to the rich man in the gospel was to join the discipleship community as they traveled along the way. The work of relinquishment is difficult for individuals to realize in isolation. In community we cultivate a common vision that facilitates relinquishment. Community gives us the support necessary to take those steps out of our comfort zones toward the margins of society.

Like that rich man in the gospel we are generous, we support the "right" causes, and we can list the laws that we have obeyed as "good, moral people." If we adopt this posture, we will never really understand the gospel invitation before us. We can invoke rational arguments for moderation and good sense against the way of Jesus and the way of Francis. This is understandable, for there is something foolish and risky, even senseless, about this path. It is even scandalous! How can a way that seems so negative promise the kind of delight, joy, and abundant life that Jesus promised and Francis found?

Once again we find ourselves invited by Francis to be fools. Is it really possible that what is given up will be returned one hundredfold? Can we believe that as we lose ourselves, we will find ourselves? Francis, who renounces his claim on all things, is free to enjoy all things as gift. Utterly foolish. Impractical. Subversive. Even dangerous.

We can neutralize the challenge and promise of Jesus and of Francis by elevating Jesus and Francis into the realm of sainthood and perfection, a realm seemingly far beyond our reach. Or we can ponder their way of living in the world and attempt to follow them, fools though we be. It is probably impossible to extract from Francis a precise formula for achieving this kind of freedom. We tell the stories of Francis and of Jesus because we cannot do what we cannot imagine. By telling these stories, may we at least come to imagine that a different way is possible; that we can actually live the gospel; that we can be free of the tyranny of possessions; that we can experience joy in the simple gifts of life and of each day; that we can surrender our lives to a purpose larger than ourselves; and that we can dare to hope for the transformation of the world. In telling the story of Francis, we place ourselves in the presence of one who, in losing his life, found it; who in giving up the world received it back transformed; who discovered Christ mysteriously hidden and revealed in the life of the poor. We dialogue with one who believed along with Jesus that with God, "all things are possible."

OUR STORIES

Reflect on your childhood and adolescence.

• What significance did having things and buying things have in your family?

• How important were material possessions, educational level, and social status in your family and community? By what values did you come to evaluate yourself and other people? Where did you get those values? What else can you remember about attitudes toward possessions and social status?

Reflect on your adult life.

• In what ways have you internalized your culture's voices regarding possessions and economic status? Have those internalized voices ever compromised your freedom to choose? Have you ever challenged those internalized attitudes?

• Recall times when you have said to yourself, "If I only had a _____, I would be happy." How has that attitude affected your ability to depend on God? or to share who you are? Do you ever respond to anger, depression, sadness, frustration, happiness, or boredom by "buying something"?

• Can you recall times when you have silently evaluated someone based upon his or her clothing, house, or other material possessions? Can you recall a time when you have been evaluated on that basis?

• In what ways have your attitudes toward material possessions changed throughout your life? Why?

• Do you have a personal relationship with anyone who has chosen to live more simply out of a religious commitment? How do you feel about that person? How has that relationship affected your life?

• Have you a personal relationship with anyone who has a great deal more material wealth than you have? How do you feel about that person? How has that relationship influenced your life?

SIGNS OF OUR TIMES

In the United States we are unaccustomed to viewing ourselves in terms of class. For most of our history, we have imagined ours to be a "classless" society, in which movement from one level of wealth or power to another was quite possible with enough hard work, enough "bootstrap pulling." Until recently, this illusion was perpetuated by the constant ability of the dominant group in society to expand, both economically and geographically. At least for those of European descent, the United States seemed truly a land of opportunity.

Beneath the egalitarian surface, however, sharp divisions have long simmered. The most pronounced of these is the vast chasm that exists between the ordinary American citizen and a small minority of very wealthy and powerful people. Recent studies confirm what the poor have known all along: that the gap is widening, the rich are getting richer and the poor are getting poorer. The gap between the richest and poorest U.S. citizens is now greater than at any time since the Census Bureau began collecting data in 1947. The poorest twenty percent of the U.S. population receive 3.8 percent of the national income; the richest twenty percent get 46.1 percent (*Brave New World Order*, Jack Nelson-Pallmeyer, Orbis Books, 1992, p. 19). African Americans, Native Americans, and other minority groups experience an increasing marginalization that has erased much of the hope engendered by the civil rights movement.

A glance at some statistics illustrates the point. According to Bread for the World's 1992 *Hunger Report*, by the end of the 1980s 32 million U.S. Americans lived on incomes below the official poverty line ($13,400 for a family of four in 1990), with 12.5 million of those living on incomes of less than $6,700 per year. Yet hunger and poverty increased in the early 90s:

> About one in five children under age eighteen lives in poverty. Under age six the rate is almost one in four. Roughly 15 percent of white, 36 percent of Hispanic, and 44 percent of African-American children live in poverty (*1992 Hunger Report*, Bread for the World Institue on Hunger and Development, 802 Rhode Island Avenue, NE, Washington, D.C. 20018, pp. 157–158).

Because so many in the United States see themselves as middle class, or know themselves to be "just making it," it is very painful and difficult for ordinary U.S. citizens to understand the significance of a global social analysis that shows them to be privileged and powerful. We emphasize the ordinary in our self-understanding and fail to recognize that we as 6 percent of the world's population consume over 40 percent of its resources, that we are better off by far than two-thirds of the world's population, and that our very lifestyles and structures often perpetuate the inequality of global relationships.

Reflect on your economic status.

• What words would you use to define your economic status?

• Consider the following: If the world were a global village of one hundred people, over seventy of them would be unable to read, and only one would have a college education. Over fifty would be suffering from malnutrition, and over thirty would live in what we call substandard housing. Six of them would be from the United States. Those six would have half of the village's entire income; the other ninety-four would exist on the other half. How would the wealthy six live "in peace" with their neighbors? Surely they would be driven to arm themselves against the other ninety-four—perhaps even to spend, as we do, more per person on military "defense" than the total personal income of the others.

• Does seeing yourself in these terms as part of the global community alter your initial response? If so, how?

• How do you view your current economic status? your level of material possessions? If your basic needs are not being met (e.g., you cannot afford health care for yourself or your family, housing or transportation costs are exceeding your income, etc.), how does that affect your self-image? How do you feel about more affluent Americans?

INVITATION TO RESPOND

In the exercise to follow, we invite you to enter into a process of self-examination and response as we look at issues of lifestyle and specifically at our resources and how we use them.

• First, list the primary people or institutions to which you are responsible. Very simply, to whom are you accountable?

• Do an inventory of the resources available to you in at least these dimensions of your life: personal/family life; parish/faith community; vocation; citizenship. Be sure to include human gifts of time and talent, economic, political, and cultural resources, and access to different circles of influence.

• Reflect on each area. Consider how your use of this resource either inhibits or supports the realization of social justice.

• If you have already made or were to make a primary commitment to the struggle for justice, what concrete impact would that commitment have on the ways in which you use the resources available to you?

• Focus on one resource area and list concrete changes that you could make that would help you to use these gifts more in the service of God's liberating activity in the world.

3

FRANCIS AND COMMUNITY

In those days he departed to the mountain to pray, and he spent the night in prayer to God. When day came, he called his disciples to himself, and from them he chose Twelve, whom he also named apostles: Simon, whom he named Peter, and his brother Andrew, James, John, Philip, Bartholomew, Matthew, Thomas, James the son of Alphaeus, Simon who was called a Zealot, and Judas the son of James, and Judas Iscariot, who became a traitor. (Luke 6:12–16)

The community of believers was of one heart and one mind ... they had everything in common. With great power the apostles bore witness to the resurrection of the Lord Jesus, and great favor was accorded them all. There was no needy person among them, for those who owned property or houses would sell them, bring the proceeds of the sale, and put them at the feet of the apostles, and they were distributed to each according to need. (Acts 4:32–35)

FRANCIS' STORY

No dramatic pathways opened for Francis immediately after his conversion. He simply took what he deemed the next right step, then the next. He began repairing rundown churches in the region of Assisi, believing that this was what the Lord wanted of him. Little did he realize that before long it would be the church universal that he would repair, in company with hundreds, then thousands, of men and women who wished to walk Francis' way. How long this period of solitude and physical activity lasted is not clear. Soon enough, however, it became apparent to the young Assisian that his was not to be the life of a hermit, but that followers would flock to his side.

Thomas Celano, the first authentic biographer of Francis, tells us about the early companions of Francis:

This [St. Damian's Church] is the blessed and holy place, where the glorious religion and most excellent order of Poor Ladies and holy virgins had its blessed origin about six years after the conversion of St. Francis and through that same blessed man. Of it the Lady Clare, a native of the city of Assisi . . . was the foundation. (Celano, VIII, 29)

Others followed:

A certain man from Assisi, of pious and simple spirit, was the first to devoutly follow the man of God. After him, Brother Bernard, embracing the delegation of peace, ran eagerly after the holy man of God to purchase the kingdom of heaven . . . (Celano, X, 24)

But immediately another man of the city of Assisi followed him; he deserves to be greatly praised for his conduct and what he began in a holy way, he completed after a short time in a more holy way. After a not very long time Brother Giles followed him; he was a simple and upright man and one fearing God . . . (Celano, X, 25)

One day when he [Francis] was wondering over the mercy of the Lord with regard to the gifts bestowed upon him, he wished that the course of his own life and that of his brothers might be shown him by the Lord; he sought out a place of prayer, as he had done so often, and he persevered there for a long time with fear and trembling standing before the Lord of the

*whole earth ... And then, coming back, he said with joy to
his brothers: "Be strengthened, dear brothers, and rejoice in
the Lord, and do not be sad because you seem so few; and
do not let either my simplicity or your own dismay you, for,
as it has been shown me in truth by the Lord, God will make
us grow into a very great multitude and will make us increase
to the ends of the world ..."* (Celano, XI, 26)

*At this same time also, when another good man had entered
their religion, their number rose to eight ...* (Celano, XII, 28)

*When blessed Francis saw that the Lord God was daily adding
to their number, he wrote for himself and his brothers, present
and to come, simply and with few words, a form of life and
rule, using for the most part the words of the holy Gospel ...
He then came to Rome with all the aforementioned brothers,
desiring very much that what he had written should be con-
firmed by the Lord Pope Innocent III.* (Celano, XIII, 30)

It is important to note once again the social melieu within
which the Franciscan community emerged. The feudal system
had seen its best (or worst) days and was quickly fading from
the European scene. City-states, the forerunners of nation-
states, began to form. Violent rivalries often marked these small
kingdoms. Indeed, Francis himself began his adult life seeking
glory as a warrior for his native Assisi. The church, with all its
medieval trappings, still held sway, the most powerful force in
that part of the world. A new middle class of tradespeople and
small landowners began to appear, with many of the virtues and
failings we see in that class today. The shifting social order
brought with it increased marginalization of the poor. A "new
grace" was needed as the times changed; the Spirit provided
this grace in Franciscan community life.

Upon his conversion Francis did not set out to gather people
around him. Initially, as noted above, his turning to the Lord
seemed to him an entirely individual experience. He went about
repairing the churches in the vicinity, spending the rest of his

time in prayer. However, God had other designs. As we have seen, one, then three, then eight men from the area came to see what Francis was about. And they stayed. Clare and her sister Agnes joined him, thereby giving birth to the Franciscan sisterhood.

So the young Francis realized that he was attracting followers and was called to provide a community structure for them. In the truest sense, the whole Franciscan charism of brother- and sisterhood came not from the "founder" but from God. People were drawn to join the Poverello by the same Spirit who inspired Francis; he did not invite them. In the prologue we have recounted the delightful story of Brother Masseo, who, much later in the life of the movement, cried out at seeing the throngs who flocked to the order: "Why after you, Francis; why after you?" To this brother's mind the phenomenon was incomprehensible.

As their community life took shape, definite characteristics began to emerge which corresponded to the signs of the times. These would mark the movement forever:

- the communities were essentially made up of laypersons, not clerics;
- Francis' followers were women as well as men;
- the communities rejected the idea of monasteries and lived among the people;
- the style of life was collegial, with those in leadership at the service of the group;
- the friars worked for their upkeep, and when that failed, they begged;
- Francis' followers rejected violence of every kind;
- they inserted themselves in the world;
- their ministry took them into the marketplace.

Finally, in their stark living of the gospel, the followers of Francis and Clare stood as a challenge to the institutional church. We can only speculate on the extent of this challenge. When one recalls the state of the Roman church in the Middle

Ages—with its pomp, wealth, corruption, patriarchy, intrigue, and power—the idea of an officially recognized order of men and women with characteristics that contrasted sharply with those of the institutional church in those times is amazing.

The first rule* of life that Francis adopted was the gospel itself, especially gospel texts that describe how Jesus' followers are to go about the world. In its zeal to imitate the historical Jesus, Francis' rule of life appears to interpret the gospel with almost fundamentalist literalness. What he was doing, however, was a creative appropriation of the gospel for his own time. The way of life he chose for his community allowed for differences between their time and that of Jesus: for example, Francis' rule of life forbade Franciscans to ride horseback as an elitist activity of that time. Yet his adherence to the gospel remained basic and all-embracing; it was the soil, the air, and the environment for the life of Franciscan communities.

Moreover, Francis' decision to use gospel texts for his rule signaled the Jesus-centeredness which was his hallmark. Francis knew that the brothers and sisters were following him, yet he turned to words of and about Another in order to formulate a rule of life to guide the band that began to form around him.

Characteristics of the Franciscan Communities

The characteristics of Francis' communities derived naturally from his own personality and vision. The most innovative may have been the *lay character* of Franciscan men's communities. Francis was not ordained a priest, nor was the group which gathered around him predominantly clerical. Though there were ordained men among these first followers and those who would come afterward, it was essentially a fraternity from the start. In this Francis followed the actions and words of Jesus at the Last Supper when he washed the feet of his disciples and charged them, "So if I, your Lord and Teacher, have washed your feet,

---

* A "rule" of life in Roman Catholic terminology refers to the regulations and guidelines that inspire and guide a particular order.

you also ought to wash one another's feet" (John 13:14).

The church of Francis' time (not unlike our own) was dominated by a clerical caste system. Church life seemed to revolve around the ordained men who ruled the lives of the laity. This unhealthy and unchristlike situation proved an increasing scandal and would provide the reformers of the fifteenth and sixteenth centuries with one of their chief criticisms of the Roman church. The emergence of a brotherhood and a sisterhood in which clerics and laity lived together as equals challenged the church to its very foundation. Despite many aberrations in living out this charism through the centuries, and attempts even today to clericalize the Franciscan order, it has remained in its ideal state a nonclerical order of brothers and sisters.

A second characteristic of the early Franciscan movement is its *inclusion of women.* Clare was among Francis' first followers; thus the young order profited from her gifts and those of the women who later followed. Francis wrote a rule of life for his brothers and it is worthy of great note that despite the paternalism of the age, he could encourage Clare to draw up guidelines for her sisters. These Poor Ladies, as they were known, came from all social classes, even the poorest. This was a departure from the norm of that day when candidates for the convent arrived with substantial dowries, which added to the wealth of the institution and thereby gave these daughters of the wealthy an even higher station in society. In tracing the characteristics of Franciscan community life, the influence of Clare can be seen clearly throughout. Francis' embrace of Clare and her sisters into the new way of life mirrors Jesus' own example when he commissioned Mary Magdalene to bear the good news of his resurrection to the disciples: "Go to my brothers and tell them" (John 20:17).

Francis' community chose not the monastery, a place removed from the world, but rather a life *dedicated to action and contemplation.* Until Francis' time men and women who wished to dedicate their lives to God as vowed people had only one choice: to leave the world and enter cloistered monasteries. This system of religious life had been in place for seven hundred years when the man of Assisi burst on the scene. In one of his great innovations, Francis broke this mold by remaining in the world. He understood his vocation to be as much in the streets announcing and acting on the good news of incarnation and salvation as spending endless hours in retirement and prayer. One story about Francis tells how he went out one day with another friar to preach. The two walked through Assisi for hours and then returned to the friary without having spoken a word. When the brother asked Francis about his intention to preach, the saint replied that their presence on the street was a sermon.

Thus was born the model of religious life that remains until today: activity flowing from contemplation; contemplation informed by activity. Religious life would never again be the same. Clare, it is true, had to retire to the cloister, since the idea of active women religious was incomprehensible at that time. Still, the fact that Clare joined Francis at the beginning and was identified with him as cofounder of the Franciscan movement surely influenced later generations of vowed women to take up an active-contemplative life. Without leaving her cloister, Clare undoubtedly had enormous influence on religious women across Europe in succeeding centuries.

The integration of the interior and exterior lives of discipleship has served as a model not only for vowed religious life in the Catholic tradition, but also for countless individuals and communities that strive to live the gospel. In this Francis must have found guidance in Jesus' prayer on behalf of all his followers the night before he died: "I am not asking you to take them out of the world, but I ask you to protect them from the evil one" (John 17:15).

Another characteristic of Franciscan communities is that they *took people where they were* and called them to an authentic living of the gospel in the way of Francis. In Francis' mind no one had to leave the married state, for example, or a particular professional calling in order to follow the Lord. Thus, in addition to the brothers who followed him to the friaries (First Order) and the women who joined Clare (Second Order), people with family, social, and professional obligations joined the community as

secular Franciscans (Third Order). Given the theology of religious life of that time, this acceptance of people's state in life as
compatible with full membership in the Franciscan family was
a radical departure from accepted ways and an entirely new
understanding of dedicated life.

As yet we may not have fully grasped or implemented the
Franciscan charism in this regard. Much ecclesiastical life still
revolves around the clergy, while the dignity and responsibility
of all baptized persons often receive but lip service in pastoral
practice. Many Christian denominations need to value the marketplace vocation as authentic and indeed as a necessary vocation to hasten the final coming of the Lord through participation
in the world's transformation (cf. 2 Peter 3:12).

Our Lord's own inclusiveness must have inspired Francis.
Jesus had disciples from all walks of life and displayed amazing
respect as well as tolerance for the concrete situations in which
people found themselves. He received a Jewish religious leader,
Nicodemus, at night when the man was too afraid to approach
Jesus in daylight. He went to the home of the rich Zaccheus and
pronounced salvation on his household. He ate in the house of
Simon the Pharisee. For Jesus, discipleship meant not so much
a drastic change of one's vocation as a totally new way of living
it out. It signified a radical conversion of heart in the life situations in which people found themselves.

Characteristically, Francis' community was *governed in a collegial manner.* Francis, the non-cleric, was of course the leader,
the founder, and the visionary. He was also "your little brother
Francis" who took care of the community as a "mother loves
and nourishes her carnal child" (Franciscan Rule of Life). While
he would rigorously defend his ideals and desires for the order,
his manner toward the brothers, even toward those who failed
to live up to the ideal, was eminently gentle. This collegiality
was not free of problems, however. As in any group, factions
arose and Francis' leadership was challenged. He once resigned
as minister general of the order. Yet ideally, and generally in
practice during Francis' life, leadership in the order was exer-
cised as a ministry to the collective. Those in positions of author-

ity, even those who would follow Francis in general leadership, were called ministers rather than superiors.* This usage is telling. It recalls Jesus' own thinking on the matter: "You know how among the Gentiles those who seem to exercise authority lord it over them; their great ones make their importance felt. It cannot be like that with you. Anyone among you who aspires to greatness must serve the rest; whoever wants to rank first among you must serve the needs of all. The Human One has not come to be served but to serve — to give his life in ransom for the many" (Mark 10:42–45).

With regard to their life in common, we can well say that these first Franciscan communities practiced exemplary love, gentleness, and forgiveness within their ranks. They bore one another's burdens and fearlessly spoke the truth to each other. The communities were *places of great joy,* where men and women lived the original charism of the one who has been called "Mirror of Christ."

Another innovation of Francis' growing communities was the custom of *begging for one's sustenance* when other forms of support proved insufficient. Religious in the monasteries had always worked to support themselves, and Francis surely carried on that tradition. He went so far as to condemn as a "Brother Fly" any brother who would not work. But, startlingly, the saint went so deeply into solidarity with the destitute that he and his brothers accompanied the poor even in the demeaning activity of begging when work failed to produce enough to live on. It serves as an example of what Leonardo Boff has called Francis' final step on his journey toward the poor: not only helping the poor, not only being in solidarity with them, but ultimately becoming poor himself. The brothers, under Francis' tutelage, went about asking for alms on behalf of the poor and for themselves. The appellation "mendicant" (beggar) thus came to describe this new kind of religious order.

---

* A *superior* in Catholic religious parlance does not connote superiority, but rather responsibility and authority in the community. Nevertheless, because of the word's etymology, it has never enjoyed widespread usage in Franciscan circles.

This cornerstone characteristic of the Franciscan community found its inspiration in the text from Luke's gospel that so influenced Francis: "Take nothing for the journey, neither walking staff nor traveling bag; no bread, no money. No one is to have two coats. Stay at whatever house you enter and proceed from there" (Luke 9:3–4).

Francis assumed a most pacifist posture: his community was *not to engage in violence* of any kind. This empowered Francis to serve as a reconciling force in situations of conflict. For example, it was Francis who mediated and eventually healed the serious rift between the bishop of Assisi and the mayor of that city; Francis who reconciled the Sultan of Egypt with Christendom. Constantly reflecting on the sufferings and death of Jesus, Francis could not but have taken this inspiration to nonviolence from Matthew's Gospel, which relates how at the moment of his arrest Jesus chided those who would defend him with violence: "Put back your sword where it belongs. Those who use the sword are sooner or later destroyed by it" (Matt. 26:52). This characteristic of Francis' community is most evident in the rule set out for lay people who wished to follow Francis but, because of their duties in life, were prohibited from actually living in a friary. On these Third Order members Francis strictly enjoined the prohibition against bearing arms.

Finally, as already noted, the emerging Franciscan community *challenged the Roman Catholic church of that time.* Initially church authorities felt uneasy about another group of "zealots" who proposed to "rebuild the church." There were quite enough of these already, and they very often signified a real threat to the institution. Gradually, however, as Francis showed himself and his band to be totally loyal to the church, he received acceptance even at the highest levels of the Roman communion. His earliest rules contained admonitions regarding obedience to bishops and to "the Lord Pope." He went to Rome early on to ask Innocent VI's formal approval of his way of life. On the other hand, his simple and concrete living of Jesus' gospel, his espousal of Lady Poverty, and his stark, almost literal imitation of the Lord proved an enormously challenging and renovating force in the church. In fact, Francis has been called the "first Protestant" because of his reform from within the body of the church. He saw such reform as always necessary, given the frailty and sinfulness of a human institution. He and his communities walked a most difficult path: remaining in a sin-filled church while offering her a prophetic challenge. He and the first communities served as a constant critique to the church, living as they did the gospel without gloss, a witness that called the entire household of faith to do the same. To the church's ostentation, inattention to the poor, neglect of pastoral responsibilities, complicity in the violence of the state, and general situation of decline, the emerging Franciscan movement offered both a strong condemnation and a corrective. It was the communal example of Francis and his followers, rather than rhetoric, which offered the critique and provided the challenge.

Jesus had given the example long before. A devout Jew, he insisted that he had come not to repeal the laws of that religion but to fulfill them. Yet his obedience to God's will and his announcement of the Reign of God proved an enormous threat to the socio-religious power structure of that day. Jesus became entirely too much for them to bear, and the Jewish authorities finally said: "If we let him go on like this, the whole world will believe in him. Then the Romans will come in and sweep away our sanctuary and our nation" (John 11:48).

Church Institutions Today

Much of Francis' genius in developing his gospel-centered communities remains sadly lacking in our churches today. Francis' appreciation of the laity, the gifts of women, his integration of contemplation and action, collegiality, simplicity of life, and rejection of violence, to name just a few, remain ideals which our modern church life has yet to attain.

Our era has been called "the age of the laity," and indeed, recent decades have seen an increase in the appreciation of the laity's contributions to the body of Christ. Yet much remains to be done. Through Baptism the laity are full members of the body of Christ, with rights and responsibilities inherent in their lay vocation. But too often, ordination to the clerical state is the source of power in the church, and lay people function at the service of, or in answer to, priests — a situation which clearly needs to change.

On the other hand, women's contributions to church life have only begun to be recognized. One wonders what Clare's place would have been had she lived today. Would her passion, intelligence, and steadfastness to the ideals she shared with Francis have been called forth now in ways that were impossible when she lived? Women today are still denied ecclesiastical equality. Their struggle for their rightful role takes place not only on a personal level, but also in relationship to church structures that are often a countersign to the gospel itself. Many Roman Catholics perceive this structural sin in the absolute denial of priestly and episcopal ordination to women.

For Francis and his followers to integrate contemplation with life in the world meant a radical departure from the normal, cloistered religious life of that time. Today, however, the single most recognizable integrating factor in Christian spirituality may be the reality of contemplation in the midst of the world. At the same time, we have much to learn in this regard. Although lip service is given to the value and importance of integrating action and contemplation, the need remains for growth in practice on the part of both contemplatives and activists.

The churches have far to go with regard to such characteristics of the Franciscan movement as collegiality, simplicity of life, and the rejection of violence. The Roman Catholic church's authoritarian spirit, which Franciscanism challenged in the thirteenth century, unfortunately remains very much with us today. Other churches, too, regard authority as privilege rather than as service. Proof of this lies in the rejoicing of the faithful when a religious authority figure genuinely assumes the role of servant or prophet. Similarly, austerity in the use of things — that overriding Franciscan trait — is practiced more by way of exception in the churches, even by members of Franciscan orders. Excessive materialism characterizes many of these groups. Further, despite good faith rhetoric and the efforts of some members, many denominations have yet to instill in their people the ideal of nonviolence and active pacifism, especially with regard to participation in war.

Wherever one looks these days, the sins of the institutional churches seem to glare at us. Perhaps reflection on the life and work of Francis in light of the present situation in our churches will serve as a much-needed impulse to action by concerned men and women of faith.

Community Today

It is clear that today, just as in the time of Francis, the Spirit is raising up countercultural Christian communities at a time when God's people most need the support and challenge such gatherings can provide. This "community of communities," as it is called, strives to live *as if* the priorities of modern society did not hold sway; *as if* the values of God's Reign were already operative in modern society. Such communities witness to the new heavens and the new earth prophesied in the book of Revelation.

The experience of Francis, though distant in history, provides a ray of hope for this new movement. Today, too, there is a need to "rebuild my church," and the rebuilding promises to take place in and through this movement of communities.

Rebuilding the church today does not involve specifically ecclesiastical issues so much as it means moving the church to confront society as a whole, like the prophets of old, and to speak the truth of God's Reign to temporal power. Quite understandably, God is calling forth groups of communities to take up today's version of Francis' vocation. The sheer size and complexities of modern life go far beyond any individual's capacity to confront it all. Thus the community becomes a crucial way of fulfilling the mission of proclaiming God's Reign on earth. The community is more than the sum of its parts when it feels itself truly in mission to a hurting world.

In communities we join with scores of faith-filled men and

women to live the great political and theological "as ifs." Politically we live *as if* our nation were still true to its foundational
documents of liberty and justice for all; *as if* people mattered in
themselves and not for their economic or social status; *as if*
consumerism and the shopping mall did not determine the
meaning of our lives; *as if* we were facing squarely the epidemic
called AIDS and mobilizing against it; *as if* we were a sister
nation among all the other countries of the world; *as if* right
made might and not the other way around. Living these "as ifs"
in the midst of community creates the prophetic possibility at a
local level, the space for modeling how things could be, ought
to be, and will be one day. The characteristics of Francis' communities on which we have been reflecting give us a formula for
such "as if" living.

Theologically, communities live *as if* God truly exists and calls
us to be cocreators of God's Reign on earth; *as if* God cared
enough about us to send the Son to share our journey on earth;
as if that true Messiah went the way of the cross and came
through it as the Risen One; *as if* that resurrection made all the
difference in the world; *as if* we really were living out this hope.

OUR STORIES

From our earliest days, all of us have formed part of communities, though we may not have recognized them or called
them that. The immediate and extended family, the neighborhood, schools we attend, formal and informal groups of which
we are a part, our social and working circles—each of these
gatherings demonstrates that we are social beings, called to live
in relationship with others.

A few people actually live in faith-based communities. Other
people of faith today actively seek a Christian community with
which to relate. Many of us have experienced church-based communities—for example, parishes, congregations, or Bible study
groups. Answer the following questions in light of the characteristics of the early Franciscan communities: gospel-based, lay,
inclusive, inserted, democratic, poor, nonviolent, and prophetic.

• What lessons for life have you learned from your participation in family, neighborhood, and other forms of community?

• Think about one or two experiences of community you have had. Were they positive? Negative? Reflect on these experiences, both the positive and the negative.

• Do you sense within yourself a longing for more intentional community among people of faith today?

SIGNS OF OUR TIMES

In many places today desire for community has intensified. Twelve-step programs, self-help, support, and therapy groups are but a few signs of this phenomenon. For people of faith, the growing awareness that the priorities of our society often stand in opposition to Christian values has produced in them a thirst for faith-based community. Many of these people become involved in or actively seek the kind of base Christian community that has burgeoned, for example, in Latin America. People of the gospel in many places search for or are actually forming communities of all kinds, such as Bible study groups, prayer circles, intentional or live-in communities, peace and justice advocates, or groups connected with national organizations such as Pax Christi or Sojourners.

Much study is being done regarding these communities. Academics, pastoral theologians, sociologists, and even secular organizations are examining the phenomenon of Christian community in the United States today.

Contemporary Need for Community

Our desire for community comes none too soon. To continue on our individualistic way, taking care of Number One, making sure "I get mine and mine get theirs," is resulting in a societal and spiritual wasteland. However we look at it—economically,

socially, politically, ecologically, theologically, or educationally —
seeking to live more in common holds the promise of a more
fully human life for ourselves and the world.

There are parallels between today's experience and Francis'
history of community. Perhaps we, like him, did not expect to
be called so insistently by the Spirit to live communally; our
course, like his, will have to be mapped as we walk it. Those
who have begun this journey know personally the difficulties
Francis encountered in the formation and nurturance of community. In our time, as in that of Francis, change comes at us
from all sides. New ways of doing things, even of being, need to
be tried, for institutions do not serve society as they should. Yet
we, like Francis, find companions also desirous of living in community.

The experience of traditional, primarily Catholic religious
orders and congregations serves as a valuable resource in the
formation of new gospel-oriented communities. The men and
women who live out the Franciscan charism, for example, are
inheritors of a centuries-old experience in living community.
Their congregations have survived for eight hundred years, and
today's members carry that memory in their corporate life. They
have observed most of what community means, are not surprised
at its unpredictability, and thereby possess much wisdom for the
communities being formed today.

At the same time, these traditional religious communities,
including Franciscans, are themselves searching for meaningful
directions in modern life. They have been told to return to their
original charisms and there find guidance for responding to the
signs of our times. Their search has proved rewarding in many
cases and painful in others. Many of their members have turned
to other pathways in life; some congregations have disappeared.
But the very search for relevance and authenticity has itself
offered a model for the new movement of the Spirit toward
community in our time. Building community is an ongoing task
rather than something to be accomplished once and for all.

Despite this search and the notable increase in numbers of
gospel-oriented communities, building and nurturing them pres-

ent formidable challenges. The phenomenon of both secular and faith-based community-building in the United States flies in the face of the destructive individualism that so marks our culture. We are driven into isolation by such fallacies as "pulling oneself up by one's bootstraps," "doing it my way," and similar popular slogans. A look at recent history has revealed the impossibility of such American ideals in the lives of so many.

Our affluent culture highlights the individual and individualism to the detriment of the collective, and all of us have internalized these values to a certain extent. This American phenomenon has been closely studied in *Habits of the Heart* by Robert Bellah and his coauthors. We do not easily join with others, especially those who are culturally, ethnically, or socially different from us. The "common good" is not a concept much celebrated in the late twentieth-century First World. Even the most intimate relationships of marriage and family in this society often rise or fall on personal convenience or, worse, self-aggrandizement. "My rights," "my goals," and "my way of doing things" signify the ultimate criteria in so many circles of relationship. It's good if it makes *me* happy, if it makes *me* feel better, if it helps *me* to improve *myself.* This U.S. attitude militates against the self-giving, the benefit of the group, and the other-oriented attitudes that community life demands. Instinctively many among us reach for a more communal experience to combat these so-called national priorities and habits.

The paraphernalia of modern life itself tend to drive people apart. The Walkman, home video, automobile, burglar alarms, the impersonal shopping mall, the "home-as-fortress" mentality—all keep us separated from one another. In addition, the overwhelming forces that surround us—powerful and centralized government, global business interests, giant media conglomerates—dwarf the individual to the point where we wonder if we are living or "being lived." Into this breach between the person and the stifling forces around him or her, the need for mediating structures—community experiences—becomes crucial.

INVITATION TO RESPOND

All of us inevitably form a part of communities: familial, working, social, worshiping. It is not common for such groupings to be intentional—that is, for them to see themselves as true communities and act on that perception. Keeping in mind the example of Francis and the possibility that a similar grace is being offered the church in our time, we are called to break free from individualism and become more intentional in living our community experiences.

This is especially true of our worshiping community. There we gather regularly to express publicly our deepest convictions about God, ourselves, and life. We profess our faith each time we join others for prayer, reflection, scripture, inspiration, and action. Why can we not pursue this communitarian aspect of liturgy by forming smaller groups for a more intense and mission-oriented life together?

Explore with the parish or congregation to which you belong the possibility of becoming a "community of communities." This would mean a different pastoral approach by church leadership. Smaller "house churches" would gather between Sundays for prayer, discussion, Bible study, and mission. On Sunday all these gatherings might congregate in an act of fellowship and universality. The richness and creativity in faith enabled by such a participative model of church has been exhibited in ecclesial base communities in Latin America and elsewhere.

In our working environment, too, the notion of community, while less common and surely more difficult than in a church environment, has possibilities. Gatherings of professional or business persons have been tried, often for the sole and somewhat restricted purpose of praying together. Less common, but quite as important, would be Christians coming together to discuss their faith life in light of the workplace. There people of faith face similar ethical and moral problems. Can we not seek one another out and form groups to discuss and assist with the ethical choices that the office, factory, boardroom, or hospital present in terms both of personal conscience and social morality?

Consider the following questions:

• Do you sense that there is a new call to or longing for community among people of faith today?

• Has there been an outward focus or mission in the communities to which you have belonged?

• Are you now involved in community? If so, why? If not, is it because of temperament, lack of a sense of calling, an inability to find a community suited to you, or another reason?

• Do you feel called to form part of an intentional Christian community? Or would you rather not be in community at this time? How does your answer sound to you in light of the Franciscan experience?

• Imagine for yourself a community as you would like to see it. What would be the ideals you would want lived out in such a community?

• Have you ever formed part of an intentional Christian community in your workplace? Think of the people who might welcome such a venture.

4

Francis and Transforming
Friendship

Six days before Passover Jesus came to Bethany, where
Lazarus was, whom Jesus had raised from the dead. They
gave a dinner for him there, and Martha served, while
Lazarus was one of those reclining at table with him. Mary
took a liter of costly perfumed oil made from genuine aro-
matic nard and anointed the feet of Jesus and dried them
with her hair; the house was filled with the fragrance of
the oil. (John 12:1–3)

When he was in Bethany reclining at table in the house of
Simon the leper, a woman came with an alabaster jar of
perfumed oil, costly genuine spikenard. She broke the alabaster jar and poured it on his head. There were some who
were indignant. "Why has there been this waste of perfumed oil? It could have been sold for more than three
hundred days' wages and the money given to the poor."
They were infuriated with her. Jesus said, "Let her alone.
Why do you make trouble for her? She has done a good
thing for me. The poor you will always have with you, and
whenever you wish you can do good to them, but you will
not always have me. She has done what she could. She has
anticipated anointing my body for burial. Amen, I say to
you, wherever the gospel is proclaimed to the whole world,
what she has done will be told in memory of her." (Mark
14:3–9)

FRANCIS' STORY

Thomas of Celano tells a story about Francis' availability for and generosity in friendship. It is included here because it illustrates the importance and gratuitousness of true friendship. Brother Riccerio imagines himself unworthy of Francis' love but discovers not only that he is already loved deeply by the Poverello, but, also that such love is neither reward nor recompense, but rather pure gift.

A certain brother, Riccerio by name, a noble by birth but even more noble in his conduct, one who loved God . . . was led by a pious spirit and a great desire to attain and possess perfectly the favor of holy father Francis; but he feared greatly that St. Francis despised him for some secret reason and therefore made him a stranger to the favor of his affection. That brother thought, in as much as he was a God-fearing man, that whomever St. Francis loved with an intimate love would merit to be worthy of the divine favor; but on the other hand, he to whom St. Francis did not show himself well disposed and kind would, he thought, incur the anger of the heavenly judge. These things that brother revolved in his mind and spoke about frequently within himself, but he did not reveal the secret of his thoughts to anyone.

For the rest, when on a certain day the blessed father was praying in his cell and brother Riccerio had come to that place, disturbed by his usual thoughts, the holy man of God became aware of his coming and of what was going on in his mind. Immediately he sent for him and said to him, "Let no temptation disturb you, son; let no thought exasperate you; for you are very dear to me . . . Come to me with confidence whenever you wish and talk with me with great familiarity." The brother was filled with the greatest admiration at this; and as a result was even more reverent; and . . . so did he begin to open wide in his trust in the mercy of God. (Celano, XVIII, 46–47)

On another occasion, at Clare's insistence and after much consideration, Francis agreed that they should share a meal. This example of friends drinking deeply of the joy of intimacy stretches our thinking about the impact of such love:

> *St. Francis had the table laid upon the naked earth as was his custom. And when meal time came, St. Francis and St. Clare sat down together, and one of the Brothers with the companion of St. Clare, and next all the other brothers, and they humbly took their places at the table. And with the first dish St. Francis began to talk of God so lovingly, with such depth, so wonderfully, that the divine fullness of love descended upon him, and all were enraptured in God. And while they were thus transported with eyes and hands lifted toward heaven, the people of Assisi and Bettona and in the neighboring towns saw that Santa Maria degli Angeli and the whole convent and woods, which then were at the side of the convent seemed to be in a great blaze.* (Jörgensen, 120)

Perhaps we can only discover the significance of intimate relationships in the lives of Jesus and Francis by intuition and implication from a few concrete details, from legends that so often reveal the soul of reality, and from our growing comprehension of the thoroughly grounded, deeply rooted humanity of each.

Jesus and Intimacy

We begin our reflections of Jesus' experience of intimacy with what might be an historical stretch. Biblical scholars are not likely to verify a claim to intimacy between Jesus and his cousin John. In fact, the New Testament portrays more vividly other relationships in Jesus' life, yet the fact that their mothers' lives were really or symbolically intertwined and that encounters between Jesus and John the Baptizer were mutually transforming suggests that elements of the interaction between them could illustrate the gift of transforming friendship.

There is an event at the outset of Jesus' public life when he and the Baptizer share an enormously powerful moment of intimacy. Jesus is passing along the banks of the Jordan river where John is baptizing and the latter points to him, saying: "Behold, the Lamb of God, who takes away the sin of the world!" (John 1:29). Given the characters of these two men, their histories, and the vocations given by God to each, this moment has special significance for Jesus. John, son of Elizabeth, is the one selected by God to "prepare the way of the Lord," the precursor sent to announce the coming of the Messiah; he is the last of the the Hebrew Scriptures prophets. Now this key figure in salvation history alludes to Isaiah 53:7 ("Like a lamb led to the slaughter or a sheep before the shearers, he was silent and opened not his mouth") to indicate to the world, and to the Lord himself, that Jesus is the one sent to make reparation for his people's sins.

The effect of John's announcement on Jesus proved dramatic. Jesus is being told by a man whom he admires and respects that the Suffering Servant of Isaiah is he, Jesus. At this moment Jesus is initiated into the tradition of the Fool by another who lived that tradition. The Suffering Servant and the Fool are one and the same. There will be in him no stately bearing to make us look at him, no appearance that will attract us to him. He will be spurned and avoided by humans, a man of suffering, accustomed to infirmity, one of those from whom people hide their faces, smitten by God, and afflicted. It will be our infirmities that he will bear, our sufferings that he will endure. Pierced for our offenses, crushed for our sins, upon him will be the chastisement that will make us whole. The Lord will lay upon him the guilt of us all (cf. Isaiah 53).

This revelation of John stuns Jesus. In a flash of insight he is told that messiahship is his; that he will walk toward Jerusalem and death; that he will carry the sins of his people and all peoples. The revelation comes from Jesus' friend, his cousin, the man willing to "decrease while he [the Messiah] increases" (John 3:30). He understands the import of what the Baptizer is saying and retreats for forty days of solitude and fasting to reflect on what it means.

Other biblical stories offer even more direct suggestions
about the role of friendship in Jesus' life. Among the most
important are the accounts of Jesus' visits to Bethany, a village
on the other side of the Mount of Olives. Recall for a moment
Jesus' visit there in the home of Mary and Martha (Luke 10:38–
42),—Jesus' "safe house" where he went to enjoy deep friendships; to explore with his friends the profound implications of
his message; to rest and be renewed—*en*couraged—to continue
his own prophetic mission; and to invite and to challenge them
to walk with him on the journey. Mary's "better part," that of
total absorption in the balm of deep friendship, may amuse
(even irk) those of us who find ourselves so often setting the
stage of life, preparing the meals, cleaning, and creating the
possibility for life to move on gracefully. But Jesus' invitation to
Martha to share in the delicious fruits of friendship gives clear
indication of the pleasure and fulfillment he experienced
therein.

In John's Gospel (11:1–44), Jesus again visits Bethany, for
"Jesus loved Martha and her sister and Lazarus" (John 11:5).
There he was confronted with the death of Lazarus:

> When Jesus saw her [Mary] weeping and the Jews who
> had come with her weeping, he became perturbed and
> deeply troubled, and said, "Where have you laid him?"
> They said to him, "Sir, come and see." And Jesus wept.
> So the Jews said, 'See how he loved him." (John 11:33–
> 36)

Beyond companionship of the sort that Jesus must have
shared with the fishermen and others who comprised the immediate community of disciples around him, the Bethany stories
highlight Jesus' celebration of life-giving intimacy with both men
and women.

Brazilian feminist theologian María Clara Bingemer, reflecting on John's story of Jesus' anointing at Bethany (12:1–3),
describes the effusive and permeating aroma of perfumed oils
as Mary pours them over Jesus' feet. Her bold intrusion, her

interruption of the way things were already arranged in terms of table fellowship, gives powerful and concrete witness to the penetrating presence of women in Jesus' life. The anointing of Jesus' feet and Mary's drying of his feet with her hair would have been extremely unusual actions in the Jewish community of Jesus' day. A woman never appeared in public with her hair unbound, and the familiar action of welcome for dinner guests was to anoint their heads, not their feet. John wanted to underscore the extraordinary display of love and gratitude contained in Mary's lavish gesture.

In Mark's (14:3–9) version of this incident (which is probably more historically accurate), an unnamed woman pours expensive perfumes over Jesus' head. Like the gesture of love and gratitude described in John's Gospel, this woman's action of anointing was in itself prophetic proclamation. This anointing with oil, the identification of the one who was to initiate the inbreaking of the Reign of God, was a dangerous action in the tense historical context of Jesus' entrance into Jerusalem. By this action, which was defended publicly by Jesus, the woman moved from a position at the margins of Jewish society onto center stage.

Ched Myers (*Binding the Strong Man*) underscores this point and notes that this dear friend of Jesus, the woman, courageously confronts the approaching death of the one she loved. The woman anoints Jesus' body in anticipation of his death, in "ideological solidarity" with the way of the cross.

One can imagine the gift that such deeply intimate encounters were in the life of the one who was soon to face the cross. At Bethany Jesus surely received encouragement and deepened his own resolve to move forward toward the final confrontation with religious and civil authority and finally to his death on the cross.

Over the objections of some who witnessed the loving action of anointing with expensive oils, Jesus defended the woman, saying that the "poor you will always have with you," a passage so often misunderstood as an excuse for avoiding actions of solidarity and the struggle for justice. However, the mission of Jesus and his followers had by that time been clearly articulated;

the divine option for the poor had been proclaimed. Perhaps Jesus was suggesting that the Reign of God must include, but is more than, the struggle for social justice—it is seen as well in moments of merciful intimacy. In fact, without the gift of intimacy, the work for social transformation can become an arid and dehumanizing exercise. The Reign of God is built within oneself, between oneself and others, and in the social structures as well. In this conversation Jesus gave particular focus to the intimate dimensions of the New Creation task.

Jesus' celebration of women was of a piece with his celebration of the marginal ones of his time, but it went beyond that. He welcomed them into the life-giving circle around him, aware that their presence was essential at the heart of the discipleship community—that without their inclusion, the shalom was not possible. He learned from women as well as from men the possibility of life-giving relationships; he relied upon them, too, for healing and courage; he explored with them the implications of his mission; he received from them the gift of accompaniment even to the foot of the cross; and he appeared first to them when he had overcome the forces of evil and risen from the dead. The mutuality of his relationships with women was symbolically but clearly documented by the evangelists. Women demanded of Jesus his healing power (the woman with an issue of blood), delighted in his attention (Mary while her sister Martha was busy about so many things), claimed his respect (the woman at the well), even challenged the ethnocentric worldview of his day (the pagan woman who insisted on a cure for her daughter)— and he reciprocated in every instance.

In Jesus one sees the results of this capacity for intimacy with both women and men. His appreciation of intimate relationships allowed him to show great tenderness to a widow whose only son had died (Luke 7:11–17). How he acted (tenderly) was as important as that he acted (politically). It made him sensitive to a woman with an embarrassing hemorrhage (Matt. 9:20–22 and parallels) and to one taken in the act of adultery (John 8:3–11).

At the same time, Jesus' capacity for enabling friendship was glue for the ones who followed him through tremendous stress for three years. His openness to love was part of his charisma, and the strength of the love he received in return helped him confront the weakness of the religious leadership of the day.

Francis and Intimacy

So it was with Francis. Surely his mother, Pia, then Clare and Jacoba,* Brothers Leo, Bernard, and Juniper, and many others nurtured in him the sensitivity for which he is so noted. So many times we read of this most disciplined and austere person breaking his fast and setting the table himself when a brother seemed at the point of utter exhaustion from want of food. We see Francis anticipating his brothers' needs, as exemplified in the story of his concern for Brother Riccerio. The Franciscan brotherhood was clearly a community of gentleness and love. In the writings of Francis,

the word brother is used more than any other (242 times), almost always accompanied by an adjective of affection: "my most beloved brothers," "my blessed brothers," "my brothers." His care and tenderness were so intense that he was loved like a "most beloved mother." And essentially that is how he acted.
(Boff, 33)

Other friendships fostered the rigorous side of his personality: Clare's witness to austerity must have deepened Francis' own embrace of a sparse religious life, while his friendship with friar Illuminato helped sustain him on the dangerous journey across enemy lines toward the Sultan of Egypt, Malik-al-Kamil, the one feared by all Christians and target of the fifth crusade. In fact, the biographies and legends of Francis suggest the possibility of deeply loving friendships in Francis' life beyond his own fraternity, especially with Clare.

---

*Jacoba, an older woman, was a close friend of Francis. Legend has it that she visited him when he was dying, bringing sweet cakes and great love.

Twelve centuries after the time of Jesus, the place of women in society had not improved, and one is easily overwhelmed by the heavily negative attitudes of Francis' day toward women and their bodies. On the one hand, Clare's journey seemed to follow some of the most apparently self-denigrating and negative traditions of Catholic religious life. The symbolic act of cutting off her hair, for example (and Francis' participation in that), as she joined the "brotherhood"* is breathtaking when considered in the light of feminist thought today. Moreover, it would seem to contradict the essence of the Franciscan insight: that all of creation (women's bodies included) is pure gift and possesses the innate capacity to glorify God. On the other hand, as we delve more deeply into Clare's appropriation of the lifestyle suggested by Francis and her articulation of that journey for and with the women of her own community, it becomes clear that Clare was a woman who pushed back the boundaries of women's religious life in her time and challenged the Franciscan brotherhood to be faithful to their own vision of poverty as well. She was clearly an extraordinary woman, and her gift to Francis was that of calling him to risk the humanizing journey of intimacy.

Clare's strength of character helped greatly to shape the community of women and men who had gathered around the Poverello. She expected from Francis respect and mutuality and he offered her both. She gave him great love and he loved her deeply in return. The legend of the flowers that bloomed in the snow—when Francis suggested that he and Clare should see each other again only when winter was over and the roses returned—symbolizes the depth and strength of their love for each other:

"Francis and Clare were never separated" means that both were so united in the same evangelical endeavor, so strongly tied to a third reality above and beyond them, the poor Christ, his Gospel, and the service of the poor, that essentially nothing

*An action common in women's religious communities until after the Second Vatican Council.

*would distance the one from the heart of the other. Both had
their heart anchored in God. Because of this, space and time
did not count for them . . . The love that they had for each
other, always excelled by the love of both for the poor and for
Christ, made them spiritual twins. When Francis had doubts
about his own vocation, he charged Clare and her sisters to
pray to God for light. And when she suffered pressures because
of the "privilege of radical poverty" . . . Francis also worried
with his whole heart.* (Boff, 31–32)

The story of the meal shared by Francis and Clare is also
fascinating, and highly symbolic. According to the biographer
Jörgensen, the shared meal was Clare's idea; she insisted that
they should have the opportunity to be immersed in the pleasure
of each other's company and friendship. This insistence was not
a weakness, but a bold response to her own instinctive understanding of the importance of intimate moments between good
friends, of the fact that the very presence of the beloved is a
tremendous gift reflective of the presence of God, and of the
need for such moments for nourishment of the spirit.

The meal was shared with others as well. This is a require-
ment for life-giving relationships: to love with open hands in
such a manner as to embrace the world, especially the world of
the marginal ones so essential to the Franciscan way. And the
bread they broke bore the fruit of communion with the Holy
One — fiery fulfillment of the deep, respectful, faithful touching
of souls that can happen in human relationships. "Love of the
one for the other bursts toward the heavens, toward God, without ceasing to be, in everything, a profoundly human love" (Boff,
32).

Francis' profoundly fulfilling relationship with Clare and his
deep friendships with the brothers may well have inspired the
beautiful masculine-feminine interplay in the Canticle of
Brother Sun. Francis composed the canticle while he was desperately ill and convalescing in a small hut next to San Damiano,
very close to Clare and her community. The integration and
wholeness of creation is reflected in the integration of masculine

and feminine in each part of creation, enabling the realization of a fullness that reflects and honors the plan of God.

Intimacy as a Source of Renewal and Joy

Anyone who has loved deeply knows how miraculously the heaviness of life can be lifted in an encounter with the beloved. The unsurmountable gift of lightness and joy is poured forth in great abundance in the context of love.

Jesus' plea to his apostles the night of his arrest that they watch one hour with him suggests his deep need for human companionship. His hour has come and he will definitely drink of the chalice poured out for him. But his soul cries out for friendship and understanding in that very situation. Twice he arouses the sleeping eleven, repeating the request for accompaniment. Had they responded, Jesus' burden, loneliness, and fears would have lessened. He would have been able to face his approaching torments knowing that his friends were with him. Friendship — intimacy — is most needed in our darkest hours and, when shared, lifts our spirits and enables us to move on.

Jesus' retreats to Bethany suggest that they renewed him. Francis and Clare sought each other's companionship when the burdens of life became unbearable. When he was desperately ill, Francis returned to San Damiano to be near Clare and her community. It was in those dark moments when he was in terrible pain, yet bathed in the light of their friendship, that he was inspired to write the Canticle of Creation, a remarkable testament to a profound renewal of his spirit.

Particularity in Friendship

Twisted interpretations of appropriate intimacy abound in our world today. At times it seems that we are expected to expose the most intimate realities of life to public view — that everyone is called to be completely intimate with everyone else. Consider the topics addressed on popular TV talk shows. Though we may not be comfortable with such exposure, we often err in the other direction, seeming reticent or afraid of genuinely intimate special relationships.

Spiritual writers, who for years have cautioned against "particular" friendships (especially in Catholic religious orders) outside of marriage, have misunderstood this dimension of love. In the lives of both Jesus and Francis, we find the capacity for special relationships revealed. Jesus visited Bethany where he found hospitality, understanding, and love with Martha, Mary, and their brother Lazarus, especially near the end as he made his way inexorably toward the Holy City and his final hours. He also had special friends among the apostles: "the disciple whom Jesus loved" (John 13:23); "he took Andrew, Peter, James and John to a high mountain and was transfigured before their eyes" (Mark 9:2); "Simon, son of John, do you love me more than these?" (John 21:15).

Francis, too, demonstrated this same capacity for particular friendships and for the loving attitude toward all of humanity, which flows from them. We can love all people only in the measure that we love particular persons well, and this Francis did. He obviously loved Clare intensely and she returned his love; theirs is one of the many great love stories among Christian saints. That Francis also loved his brothers in varying degrees only underscores the special nature of each relationship. Particularity is a hallmark of love that is neither dangerous nor inappropriate, but which enhances the lovers' capacity to embrace the rest of the world.

Intimacy as a Source of Courage

What was the significance of intimacy for the lives and mission of Jesus and Francis? What might that say in our own times?

Jesus' encounter with his cousin at Jordan's banks marked his pathway for the rest of his life. Even had Jesus through human frailty wavered in his vocation as the Lamb of God, John's example and dedication would have strengthened him. The Baptizer went to his own death for having spoken truth to power. He reminded the sinning King Herod of a moral precept and consequently was imprisoned and beheaded. With the presence in Jesus' life of such a cousin, friend, and precursor, can we not imagine his being encouraged and emboldened when his hour came?

Jesus' anointing at Bethany took place shortly before his confrontation with religious and civil authorities brought him face to face with death. His renewal at Bethany encouraged him to take the next step toward Jerusalem. The prophetic oils of the woman's love strengthened him and affirmed his commitment to the path that God had set for him.

As men and women began to gather around Francis in love and friendship, he must have found in them a new source of inspiration for his dream. Now he would not walk alone; he would be gifted with these friends who shared the vision of radical gospel living. The young Francis was encouraged by Bernard and the others to ask the Roman ecclesial authorities to approve their way of life.

Francis' friendship with Clare deepened and nourished the vision of the beloved community, with all of its prophetic dimensions, of which they were both a part. They turned to each other when the road became unbearably difficult and found in their love the possibility of taking another step.

True friendship and deep love embolden the beloved to renewed fidelity to the gospel expressed in the concrete actions and choices of life. It thrusts us toward the world, a world so often in excruciating pain. At the same time it nourishes our capacity to move through the suffering and to believe in the possibility of transformation. Intimacy is the place where grief is made bearable and where we find the strength even to face death.

Intimacy as a Source of Revolutionary Accompaniment

Jesus' friends not only sent him forth with renewed courage to Jerusalem; they also, especially the women, went with him to Calvary and beyond. So many of those men and women who followed Jesus paid dearly for their friendship with him and for the discipleship journey upon which they embarked at his invitation. First John, then Stephen, Peter, and so many others returned Jesus' great love by loving him very well—even unto death.

Such a friend for Francis was Illuminato, the friar who, according to Bonaventure, went with Francis to confront and challenge Sultan Malik-al-Kamil of Egypt. Francis surely chose him carefully because of a deep bond of trust between them. They would spend some two years together in the riskiest circumstances, facing the possibility of death.

Clare's fidelity to the gospel must have been a great challenge to Francis; together they walked toward the margins to accompany those with no choice but to dwell there. She lived the vows in the most radical sense, totally dependent on the charity of others, precluded even from begging because of the women's cloistered life. She embraced fully with Francis the poverty of those who suffered in the society of their day. Their love for each other required of them the risks of a revolutionary journey.

Friendship in the service of the New Creation is mutually enabling of radical choices to participate in the work of social transformation. It nurtures our capacity to love deeply and is a necessary inspiration without which the path of discipleship is almost impossible. It is food, blood, and life source for those who would participate in the transformation of the social structures of our world. Life-giving intimacy thrusts us toward action for social change—toward families, communities, societies, and a world constructed to enable the inbreaking of the Reign of God. The experience of love fills us with a desire for the good.

Friendship as a Place of Accountability

From prison, John the Baptizer sent disciples to ask Jesus whether he was the one who was to come or whether they were to look for another: a curious question from the friend who had already pointed to Jesus as the Lamb of God. Scholars have interpreted it in many ways. Could John's question have been a challenge to Jesus? From the desperate situation of a prison dungeon the precursor wants a sign that his perception of Jesus is correct. "Are we to look for another?" Was I foolish in pointing to you? Give an account of yourself. And Jesus does not disappoint, much less ignore his friend's plea. "Go and tell John what you have seen," he tells John's emissaries. "The blind see; the lame walk; the deaf hear; and the poor have the good news preached to them." I am fulfilling my mandate; I am carrying out your own charge; I am doing what Isaiah said the Messiah would do. Rest assured, John, and have the courage to finish your own dramatic journey. Be of good heart, my friend; our lives, yours and mine, are meaningful.

The deep love between Francis and Clare, like the friendship between Jesus and John, evoked mutual accountability to vocation and commitment. Clare left her family to follow the Poverello, and her radical interpretation of religious life must have challenged the brotherhood, even Francis himself, in return.

Our deepest friendships offer us the possibility of confronting in ourselves the inclinations to stray from the journey toward New Creation by catching a glimpse of the powers and principalities operative in our own lives. Truly loving and respectful confrontation toward genuine accountability in Christian discipleship is most possible in the safe place of intimate relationships. And intimate friendships cannot remain life-giving for long if mutual attentiveness to the demands of fidelity to the gospel is not woven into the fabric of loving interaction.

Intimate Friendship: A Place To Meet God

A wonderful passage in the Book of Genesis contains the words of Jacob upon meeting his brother, Esau: "to come into your presence is for me like coming into the presence of God" (Genesis 33:10). The fire of unbounded love offers an incomparable taste of New Creation. A song from Les Miserables repeats this lovely notion: "Take my love for love is everlasting ... And remember the truth that once was spoken, to love another person is to see the face of God."

The more deeply we experience intimacy with another person, the more likely we are to be open to the love of God. Jesus and the Magdalene, Francis and Clare did this. We simply have to put aside all of the fears and second thoughts that the offer of intimacy brings. Despite the acknowledged risks that relationships carry with them, they are from God. They have been entered into by the Clares and Francises of history and they are the one surest safeguard from the sterile individualism that so afflicts modern society.

There are important links between intimacy and spirituality, between life in God and life in another. Life in God, for example, requires an other-centeredness not unlike selfless friendship. Life in God requires that we move our centers of gravity outside of ourselves to dance the dance of life with all peoples and all of creation. Intimate friendship calls us to dance that dance with the other as well. Life in God requires that we risk all in the cosmic effort to live justly. Intimacy requires that we risk as well—in the miraculous discovery of mutually respectful, life-giving, and just relationships.

OUR STORIES

Choose one important and intimate relationship with which you have been blessed in your life and answer the following questions as you reflect upon it:

• How have I been challenged to personal growth by this relationship?

• Has this relationship pushed me out toward a suffering world or pulled me into private space?

• How did we challenge each other to be more faithful to the gospel, especially to the social dimension of the gospel?

• In what ways did I meet God through this relationship?

SIGNS OF OUR TIMES

There is perhaps no area of life in which human beings have so consistently failed to apprehend and follow the example of Jesus as the area of human relationships. Herein lies, perhaps, the fundamental problem at the heart of the social crisis. Let us look carefully at the particular characteristics of U.S. society that make intimacy difficult or impossible. Among these we might emphasize inbred patterns of domination; various forms of separation; an intense spirit of competition; the fragmentation of families and friendships by work and other activities; and the derivation of identity from occupation or possessions. There are many other forces that tear apart relationships; we all know them well.

The industrialized Christian West has deep roots in patterns of domination from which it is almost impossible to break. We are only now beginning to apprehend the horrifying consequences of our traditional behavior—from our images of God, of our relationship with God, and even of God's innate characteristics, to our patriarchal patterns of thought and communication—from our cultural roots to our political, economic, and social patterns of organization. Without honoring the dignity of others, we simply cannot foster intimacy and mutual respect in a relationship. Whenever one person dominates and the other must act in subordination, mutuality and life-giving intimacy rooted in justice are precluded.

Similarly, racism, sexism, homophobia, and religious-ethnic exclusionary behavior militate against intimacy. The barriers that separate us from other classes or groups of people ultimately separate us as well from those whom we desire to love and cherish. It is only when we open our hearts to all people, when we pull down the walls that divide us from our brothers and sisters who are different from ourselves, that we are open to intimate relationships with another as truly equal.

Until quite recently in our society, males in particular were schooled from birth until death in a competitive spirit. Lately that emphasis has been somewhat moderated; yet, in general, as a people we believe that competition brings out the best in us, be it in athletics, studies, or work. From the time our children can walk they are introduced to competitive games. Sports that are good for our bodies are used to nurture our winning spirit as well. Grades in schools are used to encourage students not only to do their best, but also to come out at the head of the class. In business we strive to climb the ladder of success and to get ahead of our competitors. And our nation, by whatever means necessary, has to believe itself to be Number One.

Surely there is a place for the spirit of competition. But in a society where the competitive spirit has gotten out of control, it may well be impossible to cherish the other because we are trying so hard to get ahead of him or her. Relationships that truly honor the other's gifts are becoming extremely rare.

The frenetic pace of life in this society has many causes. Many of us work to survive, sometimes at two or three meaningless and low-paying jobs. Others work long hours to get ahead. Still others are so dedicated to the cause for which they struggle that they never come up for air. In addition, other activities consume inordinate amounts of our time and energy. Many are worthwhile, others not. Regardless, it is a common complaint in these United States that there is no time left for leisure—even for the leisure of the relationships that would nourish our very existence. Some would say we are in a time famine.

Who we are is defined much too often by what we do or have. This phenomenon is perfectly understandable. It is what we teach each other all the time. We ask, "What do you do?" not "What do you care about?" And Madison Avenue is incredibly convincing with its lessons about having in order to be.

> The culture of lost interiority is paradoxically a culture of lost intimacy. Alone with our passive aloneness, but not in true solitude, we find that our ability to relate to other persons has atrophied. We know not how to give ourselves to the other since it is an empty fortress we call the self. And we know not how to receive the other's love, since one cannot love what one does not know. (Kavanaugh, 10)

Look with care at the advertising in magazines, on television, or in the newspaper. Keep a list of what the advertisers say you will "become" if you buy their products or if you accomplish a particular task or feat. As *Time* magazine asserts, "We are what we eat, what we build, what we buy" — or, as a bumper sticker tells us, "I shop; therefore, I am."

INVITATION TO RESPOND

Take some time to think about who you really are and about the most wonderful characteristics of someone very close to you.

• How can you learn to celebrate the other, to listen to the other in your life with care and respect?

• How can you learn to challenge each other gently toward radical discipleship?

• What choices could you make together that would move you in this direction?

5

FRANCIS AND NONVIOLENCE

Dialogue with the Enemy

*But what I say to you is, offer no resistance to injury. When
a person strikes you on the right cheek, turn and offer . . . the
other.* (Matthew 5:39)

FRANCIS' STORY

Before reading the story of Francis' journey to Malik-al-
Kamil, the sultan of Egypt, imagine the historical context.

It was 1219, during the fifth crusade. At this point in the Holy
Roman Empire war was the way of life. Warfare, not limited to
the crusades, included fierce and brutal conflict between nobles
and between cities in which the conquered city might be razed
and its inhabitants massacred or mutilated. Speaking specifically
of Assisi, one biographer of Francis writes, "Not only had war,
with its orgies and disorders, become a necessity and a habit,
but it had become the preferred occupation, the ruling passion,
and the whole life in this city." Francis himself, in his youth, set
forth as a soldier of Assisi in battle against its neighbor and
bitter enemy, Perugia. Later he served very briefly in the papal
army before receiving a vision which moved him to leave warfare
behind.

The crusades were ruthless, characterized by plunder and
slaughter, not only of Muslims, but also of Jews and any who
were considered pagans, including some Christians deemed by

the pope to be enemies of the faith. The crusades constituted a complete reversal of the early Christians' attitude toward war, participation in which was considered inconsistent with gospel ideals. The early church advocated a ministry of reconciliation and called upon its people not to return evil for evil. Forgiveness and doing good to all people were to be the norm for God's people. Nowhere in the writings of the early church was violence advocated. For nearly three hundred years the vast majority of followers of Jesus Christ adhered to that norm by refusing to shed another person's blood under any circumstance. By the time of the crusades, in dramatic contrast, the killing of the Saracens was regarded as a religious act by the Christian church. The crusades were considered a holy war, commanded and blessed by the church as fulfilling God's purpose on earth. *"Deus vult"* ("God wills it") was the slogan under which the crusaders rallied. Killing was justified by believing the enemy to be less than human; in the words of St. Bernard, "To kill a Muslim is not homicide."

Before traveling to the sultan, Francis pleaded with the Christian commander, Cardinal Pelagius, to end the fighting. Pelagius refused and, in fact, broke off diplomatic relations with the sultan. Under these circumstances Francis journeyed to the sultan, who was considered by both church and society to be the enemy chief of state.

In the thirteenth year of his religious life he made his way to Syria where he courageously surmounted all dangers in order to reach the presence of the sultan of Egypt. At that time fierce fighting was taking place between the Christians and the Moslems and the two armies were drawn up opposite each other at close quarters in the field, so that there was no means of passing safely from one to the other. The sultan had decreed that anyone who brought him the head of a Christian should be rewarded with a Byzantine gold piece. However, Francis, the knight of Christ, was undaunted and had high hopes that he would soon realize his ambition . . .

He took with him as his companion a friar named Illu-

*minatus who was an enlightened man of great virtue, and as
they set out on their way they met two lambs. The saint was
overjoyed at the sight of them and he told his companions,
"Place all your trust in God, because the words of the Gospel
will be fulfilled in us, 'Remember, I am sending you out to be
like sheep among wolves' (Matthew 10, 16)." When they had
gone farther, they were met by men of the sultan's army who
fell upon them like wolves upon sheep and seized them fiercely.
They ill-treated them savagely and insulted them, beating them
and putting them in chains. Then, exhausted as they were by
the ill-treatment they had received, they were dragged before
the sultan by God's providence, just as Francis wished. The
sultan asked them by whom and why and in what capacity
they had been sent, and how they got there; but Francis replied
intrepidly that they had been sent by God, not by man, to
show him and his subjects the way of salvation and proclaim
the truth of the Gospel message.*

*When the sultan saw his enthusiasm and courage, he lis-
tened to him willingly and pressed him to stay with him . . .
Then he offered Francis a number of valuable presents, but
the saint was anxious only for the salvation of souls; he had
no interest in the things of the earth and so he scorned them
all as if they were so much dust. The sultan was lost in admiration at the sight of such perfect disregard for worldly wealth
and he felt greater respect than ever for the saint. He refused,
or perhaps did not dare, to become a Christian, but at the
same time he implored the saint to take the gifts and give them
to the Christian poor or to churches, for his salvation. Francis,
however, did not want to be bothered with money.* (St. Bonaventure, 702–705)

Francis returned to his community in the summer of 1220.
The entire journey lasted for a little over one year.

In a time and place in which armed conflict "had become the
ruling passion, the whole life," Francis proceeded into the
enemy camp unarmed and filled with passionate brotherly love
for the "enemy."

As we reflect upon this narrative we seek to understand Francis' profound commitment to nonviolence; and we seek guidance regarding nonviolent relationships with people defined by society as enemies, as well as with personal enemies and the enemy within the self. Francis leads us to approach the issue of nonviolence on the political, interpersonal, and intrapersonal levels, which are inextricably related to each other.

Facing the Enemy

The most salient aspect of Francis' encounter with the sultan is that Francis, in the midst of wartime, went to the enemy *unarmed* and *loved the enemy as a brother*. According to the French priest Jacques de Vitry, the only primary witness who left an account of the meeting, Francis came to the sultan as a brother: "His passionate love urged him on." Francis was indeed overwhelmingly enthusiastic in his commitment to reach out to the sultan as a brother, willing to risk his life to face him.

Francis' only rule for life was the gospel. Thus his unarmed approach, his brotherly love for the sultan, and his extraordinary capacity to contradict cultural norms reflected his understanding of how Christ would have faced the sultan. Francis writes, "The Lord says, 'Love your enemies' " (*Later Rule*, Chapter X and Admonitions). And he quotes Matthew 5:39, "Resist not evil" (*Earlier Rule*, Chapter XIV). Meeting the sultan, Francis lived the truth of the gospel message.

Francis challenges us to examine how we face those whom our nation names "the enemy." New Testament theologian Walter Wink has contributed tremendously to a theological understanding of "facing the enemy." His discussion revolves around Matthew 5:39 and is grounded in nonviolence and love of enemy. Wink reveals a deeper and more accurate understanding of the Hebrew *anthistemi*, commonly translated as "resist not":

> There is in fact no other way to God for our time but through the enemy, for loving the enemy has become the key both to human survival in the nuclear age and to personal transformation. (Wink, 1986, 15)

Biologically we are provided with only two ways of deal-
ing with our enemies: fight or flight. Jesus offers a third
way of creative nonviolence that is as relevant to international relations as it is to personal transformation. The
heart of Jesus' third way is contained in the statement in
Matthew 5:39, "Resist not evil" (KJV) or "Do not resist
one who is evil" (RSV). These translations of 'anthistemi'
are more confusing than helpful. They seem to suggest that
only two alternatives exist, violence or submission, and that
Jesus counsels submission. One either resists, or resists
not. If Jesus commands us not to resist, he would appear
to be advocating submissiveness in the face of evil. "Resist
not" thus seems to encourage passivity, weakness, and victim behavior in the face of malignant and intolerable evil.
Translated thus, Christians become doormats to be walked
on, remaining silent in the face of injustice. Jesus' real
intention is utterly lost, and the church becomes complicit
with the oppressors. (Wink, 1987, 30)

Jesus' point is altogether different. His own life is the
clearest refutation of that reading of the passage. What he
means is, "Do not resist an evil by letting the evil itself
dictate the terms of your response." ... Jesus does not
mean that we should not attempt to counter evil but that
we should not counter it with violence. (Wink, 1986, 15)

Jesus indeed modeled a third way. Clearly he did not respond
passively in the face of violence; rather, by word and deed he
resisted the violence of unjust social structures. He defied laws
and rituals that marginalized the poor and ethnic outsiders, proclaimed release to the captives and liberation to the oppressed,
extended the messianic message of liberation to the outcasts,
and favored the poor. Yet his resistance was always nonviolent.
He refused violence even as a final resort to save his life. Instead
he loved even those who would kill him: "Forgive them for they
know not what they do." Simply that.
The heart of this third way established by Jesus and followed

by Francis is love of enemy, replacing enmity with brotherhood and sisterhood. In loving those called "enemy," we recognize that they are as human as we are: they have hopes, dreams, joys, agonies; probably believe themselves to be right; and may be as threatened by us as we are by them. We realize that they, too, are children of God: that they are treasured, tenderly loved, and forgiven by God no less than we are. To identify the enemy with absolute evil is to deny that they are as human as we and that they, too, have a part of God within them.

An eloquent contemporary statement of love for enemies and nonviolent resistance is that of Dr. Martin Luther King, Jr.:

> To our most bitter opponents we say: "Throw us in jail and we will still love you. Bomb our houses and threaten our children and we will still love you. Send your hooded perpetrators of violence into our communities at the midnight hour and beat us and leave us half dead, and we shall still love you. But be ye assured that we will wear you down by our capacity to suffer. One day we shall win freedom, but not only for ourselves. We shall so appeal to your heart and conscience that we shall win you in the process, and our victory will be a double victory." (Wink, 1987, 30)

Enemy-Making

Francis' example invites us to look at the ancient human propensity for enemy-making. Individually and collectively we enable and accept violence against others by first making them into enemies in our minds, or much more subtly by perceiving others as less worthy or less human than we are.

Our inclination upon encountering people, whether individuals, groups, or nations, who are different from ourselves is not to discover who they are but to classify them, stereotype them, and draw conclusions about them based upon our belief systems. Usually we put others into one of two broad categories — us or them. "Us" consists of people with whom we identify. "Them" are those we consider different. We tend to be biased toward "us."

This dynamic becomes dangerous if we consider "them" not only different but also threatening, hostile, irrelevant, unworthy, or less human than we are. Such perceptions provide moral justification for not allocating resources to "them" and for hurting, ignoring, making scapegoats of, or even killing "them." The psychological process by which we come to believe it unnecessary to treat all people according to the same moral standards is called "moral exclusion." On a societal level moral exclusion fuels racism, sexism, classism, and war. It is engendered by negative images of "them."

The Christian church in the time of Francis attributed to the Muslims many negative images that fueled the fervor against them. Francis undermined this powerful root of enemy-making by refusing to accept enemy images of the sultan and of the Islamic people.

Today, too, exaggerated negative images of an adversary nation are used to generate public support for warfare or other policies that would seem unacceptable if the public saw the adversary in more real terms. In *Faces of the Enemy: Toward a Psychology of Enmity*, Sam Keen reveals four types of enemy images that contemporary nations paint in order to justify warfare. These images appear not only in government propaganda, but also on the screen, in print media, and in textbooks.

— The enemy is the force of evil. Wars are portrayed as battles between the forces of good and evil. Every war is a "just war" necessary to triumph over evil, the atheist enemy. Consider the words used by U.S. administrations to describe Saddam Hussein, the Sandinistas, Fidel Castro, the former Soviet Union.

— The enemy is barbaric, brutish, unattractive, cruel, and unattached to family or meaningful personal life. During World War II African-American soldiers were portrayed by the Nazis as semi-gorillas. How were the North Vietnamese depicted by the U.S.? United States soldiers interviewed by the *New York Times* during the invasion of Iraq said that in order to be effective they avoided thinking of their targets as men with families and children.

— The enemy is a rapist and seducer of "our" women. Nazi propaganda showed Jews lurking in the shadows to seduce Aryan girls. KKK propaganda depicted black men with an insatiable lust for white women. That propaganda seems distant to us now. Yet how different is it from the Willie Horton ads in George Bush's 1988 election campaign? Or from the image of Arab men "taking" Western women, which still frequents the screen?

— The enemy is portrayed as insect, reptile, or beast to justify indiscriminate slaughter. Remember the "turkey shoot" in which United States forces massacred retreating Iraqi soldiers at the end of the Persian Gulf War.

Facing the Demons Within

One root of enemy-making lies within us. We project onto others, onto "the enemy," the broken or disowned parts of ourselves and our capacity for evil in order to avoid consciousness of these aspects of ourselves. As expressed by Walter Wink, "My enemy is my mirror. I project onto my enemy everything in myself that I cannot stand, tolerate, acknowledge, or accept. My enemy returns the compliment" (Wink, 1987, 30).

This we do as individuals, as groups, and as nations. For years the United States projected evil characteristics onto "Communists" while failing to acknowledge some of those same characteristics in our own body politic. Are "evil empires" to the south emerging in our nation's collective consciousness now that the Communist threat has eroded? We are erecting on our border with Mexico a "technological Berlin Wall." Technology used during the Vietnam War and deadly force are employed to prevent Mexicans and Central Americans from crossing. The United States Marines, National Guard, Border Patrol, Drug Enforcement Agency, and Customs all patrol the border. What do we see in our neighbors to the south that necessitates this militarization of our common border?

Francis was free from enemy-making. Where others created enemies, he created brothers and sisters. He could do this because he had faced the negative elements within himself. Francis' power as a mediator, reconciler, and bringer of peace was grounded in part in his integration of the negative and the positive aspects of his being. Leonardo Boff, in his discussion of Francis as a model of integration, provides valuable insight:

> *Within every heart abide angels and demons; a volcanic passion shows itself in every human action; life and death instincts abound within every person; desires to reach out, desires of communion with others and of self-giving live alongside the urges of selfishness, of rejection, of meanness. This is especially true of the lives of the saints. If they are saints, it is because they sense all of this not as destructive; but rather, overcoming them by facing them, checking and channeling them toward the good . . . This agonizing situation can be observed especially in the person of Saint Francis . . . Francis was a saint who integrated the totality of his energies in an archetypal way. The negative especially was included . . . We believe that Francis — with his perfect joy, with his path of joyful humility, lived within the dark of the senses and spirit — may evoke in us unsuspected powers of harmony and conquest within our own heart . . . Francis, with this explicit ownership of the diabolic, liberates himself for a total experience of his own reality and so allows for an integration without rejection.* (Boff, 131, 134, 135)

For Francis, fully and humbly facing the demons within himself was a doorway into a deeper encounter with an infinitely loving God. It brought him face to face with God's mercy, boundless love, and grace, which are ever more abundant than sin.

Francis invites those of us who would be peacemakers to explore our personal inner landscapes through prayer, meditation, honest self-examination, and inner healing. Trusting that God's love for us truly is unconditional — and cannot be lessened by any inner demon — opens the door for this process. Until we begin to uncover and forgive the demons within — those parts of self that are broken, hidden, degraded, or impotent—those demons will express themselves in destructive ways. They will despise, ridicule, or hurt others. They may pull us into self-deprecation. They will lead us to create enemies and be vulnerable to enemy-images suggested to us. Acknowledging and forgiving the demons within disarms them, taking away their power for sabotaging our loving self. As stated by Rollo May, "To be able to feel and live fully the capacity for gentle love demands a confrontation with the demonic. The two appear to be opposed, but if one is denied the other is also lost" (quoted in Boff, 133).

In like manner, we must come to grips as a nation, with the demons of our history and our current life. We must uncover, acknowledge, and repent of brutal aspects of our national life that we minimize or hide through the selective writing of history. Without doing so we cannot create a future in which nonviolence and brother- or sisterhood between "enemies" is possible. The unacknowledged demons of our collective life will cripple us and others as surely as will the demons of our inner lives if we do not face them.

We might begin this process by acknowledging some of the unconscious assumptions that supported the conquest of the Americas beginning five hundred years ago. Because the presence, power, and falsehood of these "cultural myths" remain inadequately challenged, they continue to cause incalculable violence and human suffering. For example, on some deep level we, as a society, believe that:

- God was/is on the side of white Americans;
- the predominant and rightful role of people of color was/ is to support white people;
- Europeans, at the time of their arrival in the Americas, were more intelligent, articulate, sophisticated, religious, indeed more human, than were Native Americans or Africans;
- Euro-Americans had/have the right to land and natural resources upon which others had/have depended for their lives for centuries.

Defying Cultural Violence

Francis' nonviolent approach to the sultan was diametrically opposed to the mindset of both society and church. It was, after all, a stirring sermon by Pope Urban II that first inspired this "holy war" against the enemy. Although immersed in a cultural milieu that perceived and depicted the sultan as an enemy to be killed in the name of God, Francis refused to accept this image. Instead he implored political leaders to stop waging war, and he loved those whom his nation defined as enemy.

What would Francis do were he a citizen of the United States today? Whom does our nation define as enemy? What would it mean to love them as brothers and sisters? Upon whom are we waging war? What would it mean to implore our leaders to cease doing so? Can Francis teach us to uncover and refute the enemy images given to us by secular society as well as by the church? What truth would we find about those named by our society as enemy if we allowed the Spirit to lead us as did Francis? Francis' approach to the sultan constituted a repudiation of the holy war mentality of his time. What have been the "holy wars" in our lifetime? What would it mean to repudiate them?

Terrifying and enormously difficult is the challenge presented to contemporary Christians by the examples of Jesus and Francis. Are we also to reject violence at all costs? Are we to refuse use of a deadly weapon against an invader in our home even if it means loss of our own life or the life of a loved one? Are we to refuse participation in weapons production even if it means losing our savings or our livelihood? This challenge is so very difficult because it means swimming against a tremendously powerful current; it means defying the world as we know it.

We, as Francis, live in a society in which violence, both subtle and blatant, is the norm, the way of life, and in some cases even lauded. The American public applauded "Desert Storm," our nation's most violent public act in years. From our earliest years we are immersed in affirmation and glorification of violence. Note what our children are exposed to daily. Saturday morning cartoons wreak violence. Ninja turtles, glorious to five-year-olds, appear on lunch pails and notebooks, in cereal boxes and Christmas packages, in dreams and in the playground. Whether our children are destroying the "bad guys," shooting soldiers, or cheering fighter jets soaring across the screen, young minds (particularly young boys) are being trained to kill in the most proficient manner possible. Indeed, the challenge of Christ and of Francis is difficult, because to choose nonviolence at all costs means to live in ways diametrically opposed to those of our society.

The biblical mandate to "resist not evil" raises an even harder question. Are we, following Jesus, called to oppose violent social structures — the violence of a federal budget that stockpiles weapons of mass destruction instead of providing health care, education and homes; the violence of regressive tax structures that allow the rich to grow richer while infant mortality in our nation's capital rises above that of many "third-world" countries? Choosing against violence means that we can no longer ignore or accept the violence of poverty, racism, sexism, militarism, unbridled capitalism, and other forms of systemic oppression — a frightening choice indeed for the non-poor. It leads to the relinquishment of some advantages. It leads to lifestyle choices that others may find strange or threatening. It means devoting time, intelligence, and energy to efforts to confront and change structural violence.

As we experience the difficulty and the fear that accompany this challenge, we are reminded that it is probably not possible to retain a comfortable place in this world and at the same time to follow Christ. Kierkegaard calls the desire to maintain respectability and worldly honor while calling oneself a Christian "wanting to have a mouthful of flour and to blow." Christ does not promise peace as the world knows it. What better model can there be for opposing society's demands than Francis?

Loving the Enemy

We could consider Francis' model of loving the enemy to be beyond our grasp. Doing so would deny the power of the Holy

Spirit within us. In Hebrew the word for spirit, *ruach*, means not only the breath of life blown by God upon Adam but also "the wind as a force that can push and drive human beings, overcome them and carry them off, that may ambush or fall upon them and inspire them to words or deeds that far surpass their ordinary capacities." The Spirit that impassioned Francis is also with us. In the face of persecution, grief, hatred, and violent behavior God's unfathomable, forgiving love can enter us and free us from hatred unto forgiveness and even unto love for the enemy. Aided by scripture, the community of believers, and prayer, we too may be empowered by the Spirit to move beyond our human capabilities to see our enemies and those defined as enemy by our nation as brothers and sisters.

When We Are the Enemy

When we read we tend to ask, often unconsciously, "What character(s) am I in this story?" In reflecting on this narrative we have identified ourselves with Francis. Let us revisit the cast of characters and bring them into our contemporary context. What roles do we play? Perhaps some of us indeed have loved those defined as our enemies. Yet those of us who are Euro-Americans also have played a less noble role. Through our nation's foreign policy we have raided the resources of the Third World. We have waged warfare in the name of God. We are, in our own time and place, a crusader culture. Recasting ourselves in this role as we look at the story of Francis and the sultan invites us to acknowledge ourselves as the enemy of others. Our human tendency is to see ourselves as the good guys. Yet we must learn to acknowledge where we are the wrongdoers if we are to correct personal and social injustice.

The sultan's treatment of Francis beckons us a step further. Francis, although a representative of the sultan's enemy, was ultimately treated with respect, tremendous generosity, and kindness by the sultan. In what areas are we being treated respectfully and kindly by people who could choose instead to retaliate against us for wrong that we have done them? Where are we given kindness by people our country has violated? These are difficult questions. It is hard to see ourselves in the position of "bad guys" to whom a person or a people is offering the hand of forgiveness—a person or people daring to walk closer to Christ than are we. Consider many Nicaraguans who, having suffered indescribable anguish at the hand of the United States, are able to welcome U.S. citizens with words of forgiveness. Or consider many Native Americans who, knowing full well the genocide suffered by their people at the hands of Euro-Americans, still choose to accept the latter as brothers and sisters. Consider analogous examples in your personal life. Could we be moved to deeper compassion by acknowledging the sisterhood and brotherhood that has been extended to us by people who could have treated us as enemies?

The Transforming Power of Non-Violence

Finally, this encounter offers fascinating and hopeful insight into the transforming power of nonviolence and love for enemy. Both Francis and the sultan were changed for the better by each other. Francis' understanding of worship and prayer was deepened by the sultan. The sultan, who had paid gold for the heads of Christians, listened to Francis with intensity, passion, and respect. He protected Francis and his brothers by placing them under his personal security and providing them safe-conduct through the Muslim states. In fact, two firsthand accounts indicate that the sultan became extraordinarily humane to Christian prisoners of war—caring for them, protecting them, treating those who were ill, feeding them well, and releasing them. In the words of one Christian prisoner who described the sultan after Francis' encounter with him, "Such kindness to enemy prisoners has never before been recorded." Can you recall contemporary examples of the transforming power of nonviolence?

Living in a society in which the violence of racism is pervasive, we ask what Francis' approach to the sultan teaches us about nonviolence between cultures. Francis respected, learned from, and was changed by the Muslim culture. Commentaries indicate that he did not insult the sultan's religion by contradicting Mohammed. He respected Islam as venerating the same God but communicated that he believed Christianity to be more pleasing to God. Francis' letters upon his return indicate that he was impressed by the Muslims' custom of falling prostrate in the evening to praise the Almighty; he urged Christians to adopt a similar practice. Having refused the riches offered to him by the sultan, Francis did accept one gift — an ivory horn used by the muezzin to call the faithful to prayer. (The muezzin is the crier who intones the summons to prayer five times daily at stated hours.) Out of respect for the religious significance of the horn, Francis later used it to summon people for prayer and preaching. In other words, Francis did no violence to the reality of the other culture and he allowed himself to grow as a result of the encounter. What has been contemporary Western Christianity's treatment of other religions and other cultures? How do we respond personally to people from other cultural backgrounds?

OUR STORIES

Recall a time in your life when you or someone you loved was considered an outsider or even an enemy. (For example, you may have been taunted or excluded for being disabled, single, divorced, fat, ugly, unemployed, gay or lesbian, not well enough educated, too old, the "wrong" color, not part of the "popular crowd.")

• How were you perceived in relationship to the "insiders"? How could you tell? What was the impact on you? How did you feel? What did you do?

• When has your life been touched by violence? Who have been enemies in your life? Have you ever acted nonviolently where violence was expected? Have you ever befriended an enemy? What was the impact on you? What did you think and feel? What was the impact on others?

• What have been demons within yourself? Have they ever led you to harm yourself or others? Have you faced those demons? If so, has facing them led you to a deeper encounter with God?

• Have you ever confronted societal violence? What was the impact on you? on others?

SIGNS OF OUR TIMES

If possible, do this social analysis with other people.

How does "enemy-making" happen? Are we involved? What are the results? Who benefits? Who loses? What can we do to break the habit of enemy-making, as individuals and as a society? Before beginning this exercise remember that "enemy-making" refers to the dynamic of *perceiving* others in such a way that it becomes acceptable to hurt, ignore, or kill them. We are not talking about people's intentions toward us. This is not to deny that others actually may have ill intentions toward us; but the issue is *how we think about others* that may lead to conflict, oppression, war, or abuse.

Francis' encounter with the sultan is particularly relevant in light of the 1990–91 Persian Gulf War. Let us examine the concepts of nonviolence and of "enemy-making" vis-à-vis our society's treatment of Arab peoples. During and following the Persian Gulf War the United States government and news media presented distorted images of the Arab world and of Islam. These images fueled hostility against Iraq's President Saddam Hussein and helped legitimize the U.S. invasion of Iraq.

Reflect on the following questions.

• What are some of the attributes that the U. S. administration ascribed to Iraq and to Saddam Hussein? What words were used? What images were elicited?

• To whom was Hussein compared, implicitly or explicitly?

• What was achieved by these images of Hussein and Iraq?

• Do any of these images fit the categories suggested by Sam Keen: force of evil, barbarian, rapist, animal? (For example, U.S. military leaders referred to the mass shooting of the Iraqi army as it retreated from Kuwait as a "turkey shoot." What was the effect of referring to the massacred human beings as turkeys?)

• What words and images were used by the U.S. administration to describe the United States and its allies in this conflict? Did they include imagery of the forces of good or God against those of evil? (For example, an aide to General Schwarzkopf was quoted in *The Washington Post* as saying, "The nations bombing together is like a great chorus singing in harmony." He was speaking of the most pulverizing aerial bombardment in human history. What does this statement accomplish?)

• What was the impact of these images on public policy? on public opinion?

• The United States claimed "bloodless victory." Yet hundreds of thousands of Arab people died and continue to die as a result of the Persian Gulf War. What is the purpose and effect of naming it a "bloodless victory"? Does the use of this term indicate that the United States engaged in the process of "moral exclusion"?

• What about the timing of enemy-making? What purpose was served by the timing of enemy-making in this conflict? The United States had previously supported Hussein for years while he committed heinous crimes against the people of Iraq and knowing that he had killed 20,000 Kurds with chemical weapons.

These distortions were believable because they mirrored the racist images of Arabs and Muslims that have frequented print and screen in the United States for decades. Arabs and Muslims are often vilified as uncivilized, ruthless peoples who are double-dealing in their relations with other nations. According to the stereotype, they wage holy wars and are guided not by moral principles but by treachery, violence, and self-interest. Racist images of Arab men appear primarily in three forms: as corrupt, greedy oil sheiks, as barbaric terrorists, or as oversexed and lusting after Western women. People of the Islamic faith often are portrayed as very emotional, religiously fanatical, and prone to martyrdom and suicide. In the world of Hollywood, Arabs seem to have become the new savages — cruel, barbaric, greedy, sex-crazed, disliked, and without character or family values.

Images that fuel racism are not all overt; some are indirect. If an Arab American is accused of a crime, it is standard newspaper practice to identify his or her ethnic group. Such ethnic identification is hardly ever, if at all, extended to Euro-Americans. An article in *The Washington Post* described discrimination against Arab Americans.

On August 8, as U.S. troops began arriving in Saudi Arabia, the Los Angeles office of the American-Arab Anti-Discrimination Committee found a threatening message on its answering machine. Among other things it linked Arabs to excrement and Arab women to prostitution. This is the same ADC chapter where, five years ago, poet and activist Alex Odeh was killed when a bomb exploded in his office.

A few days later a doctor of Arab descent in San Francisco was interviewed by a newspaper on the situation in Iraq and Kuwait. He quickly received a letter threatening his life and the lives of his children.

An Arab-American newspaper editor in Detroit was told by a caller that if Americans in Kuwait were harmed, "I will kill you." On the same day, an Arab-American businessman in Toledo was beaten up by a group of bigots who, between punches, referred to events in the Mideast.

It didn't matter that these people, whose victimization is reported in ADC's violence log, are Americans. Instead, they have become stereotypical "Ay-rabs." Such hate crimes, including bombings, beatings, murder threats, window smashings and racist graffiti, rise steeply when the Mideast is in turmoil. In the wake of the Achille Lauro hijacking, Americans of Arab heritage became Palestinian terrorists; after the bombing of Libya, they became Libyan "fanatics." For the prejudiced, all Arabs, including Americans with Arab roots, have now become so many "camel jockeys," "ragheads," and "sandsuckers."

Such violence, whether in deed or language, obviously arises from stereotyping. Insidious portraits of Arabs are in fact embedded in the American psyche. For decades image-makers, particularly motion picture and television writers, have perpetuated these negative Arab images.

Plato recognized the power of fiction when he asserted, "Those who tell the stories also rule society." In more recent times, communications scholar George Gerbner has noted that "If you can control the story-telling of a nation, you don't have to worry about who makes the laws."

More than 400 feature films and scores of television programs have shaped Arab portraits. Their audiences have been bombarded with rigid, repetitive and repulsive depictions that demonize and delegitimize the Arab.

I recently asked 293 secondary school teachers from five states — Massachusetts, North Carolina, Arkansas, West Virginia and Wisconsin — to write down the names of any humane or heroic screen Arab they had seen. Five noted past portraits of Ali Baba and Sinbad; one mentioned Omar Sharif and "those Arabs" in "Lion of the Desert" and "The Wind and the Lion." The remaining 287 teachers wrote, "None." (Shaheen, August 19, 1990)

Reflect on the following questions:

• Do you think that this kind of stereotyping helps make warfare appear acceptable? Does it contribute to the incidence of "hate crimes"?

• What are other consequences of pervasive racial stereotyping?

• Do you think that this racial stereotyping contradicts the Christian mandate to love your neighbor? In 1989, well before the Persian Gulf crisis, a war game for personal computers was released. "F-15 Strike Eagle," unlike other electronic war games in which the enemy is anonymous, identifies the enemy to be killed as specific Arab nations. Sale of the game, produced by Micropose Software Inc., jumped by 70 percent during the Persian Gulf War. What might be the impact of this game on the attitudes and behavior of the children who play it?

• How could we as a society begin to stop "enemy-making" against Arab and Muslim people?

• What steps could you as an individual or a group take to counter stereotyping of Arabs and Muslims?

INVITATION TO RESPOND

If possible do these two exercises with other people.

• Think of a nation or group that our government perceives as enemy, portrays as enemy, and approaches violently. Recall the words and example of Christ regarding enemies. Take a moment to hear Christ's words and example as an invitation to accept the power of the Spirit. Learning from Francis, what could you do to plead for this violence to stop? to approach this "enemy" unarmed? to show brotherly or sisterly love toward this "enemy"? What economic gains do you reap from your nation's violence? What could you do to refuse those economic benefits? How could you get to know this "enemy" enough to learn from them? Now dare to commit yourself to some or all of these actions, remembering that you are empowered by the Spirit to love in ways not humanly possible.

• Consider the violence of extreme poverty in our society today, poverty which in fact can lead to death by many means. Think of the many ways in which the violence of poverty is perpetrated. Focus for a moment on how culturally "normal" it is to accept the presence of extreme poverty in this nation of wealth. What images of poor people do we as a nation have that enable us to accept dehumanizing and deadly extremes of poverty? Now remember Christ's invitation to nonviolent resistance. Name two or three steps that you can take with other people to resist the dehumanization of people who are poor. Name two or three steps you could take to resist the violence of poverty. Again, dare to commit yourself to these steps.

6

FRANCIS AND CREATION

Dialogue with the Source of All Being

The heavens declare the glory of God,
    and the firmament proclaims his handiwork.
Day pours out the word to day,
    and night to night imparts knowledge;
Not a word nor a discourse
    whose voice is not heard;
Through all the earth their voice resounds,
    and to the ends of the world, their message.
(Ps. 19:1–5)

We know that all creation is groaning in labor pains even until now; and not only that, but we ourselves, who have the first fruits of the Spirit, we also groan within ourselves as we wait for adoption, the redemption of our bodies. For in hope we were saved. (Rom. 8:22–24)

FRANCIS' STORY

The countryside around Assisi in which Francis grew up was very important to him. Early on he had a great love for the farmlands around the city and also for the wilderness of mountain, river, and forest. This great love for the natural world shaped the identity of Francis, the expression of his spirituality and mission.

There are many stories of Francis and his encounters with the natural world: with animals, birds, fish, and even insects. He walked reverently on stones; he rejoiced in the sounds of running water or blowing wind. Francis had a special love for living creatures, and they seemed to sense in him a gentle, loving presence.

Above all, as Francis' turning to God unfolded and he was gripped by the fact of the incarnation, nature became holy for him. Everything created by God had also been touched by the presence of the Word made flesh. Francis, then, was not only a lover of nature and a poet who saw great beauty in all that was around him. Much more deeply he was enthralled by God's presence in the created order.

Meanwhile, while many were joining the brothers, as was said, the most blessed father Francis was making a trip through the Spoleto valley. He came to a certain place near Bevagna where a very great number of birds of various kinds had congregated, namely doves, crows, and some others popularly called daws. When the most blessed servant of God, Francis, saw them, being a man of very great fervor and great tenderness toward lower and irrational creatures, he left his companions in the road and ran eagerly toward the birds.

When he was close enough to them, seeing that they were waiting expectantly for him, he greeted them in his usual way. But, not a little surprised that the birds did not rise in flight, as they usually do, he was filled with great joy and humbly begged them to listen to the word of God. Among the many things he spoke to them were these words that he added: "My brothers, birds, you should praise your Creator very much and always love God; God gave you feathers to clothe you, wings so that you can fly, and whatever else was necessary for you. God made you noble among all creatures, and God gave you a home in the purity of the air; though you neither sow nor reap, God nevertheless protects and governs you without any solicitude on your part."

At these words, as Francis himself used to say and those too who were with him, the birds, rejoicing in a wonderful way according to their nature, began to stretch their necks, extend their wings, open their mouths and gaze at him. And Francis, passing through their midst, went on his way and returned, touching their heads and bodies with his tunic. Finally he blessed them, and then, after he had made the sign of the cross over them, he gave them permission to fly away to some other place. (Celano, XXI, 53–54)

How great a gladness do you think the beauty of the flowers brought to his mind when he saw the shape of their beauty and perceived the odor of their sweetness? He used to turn the eye of consideration immediately to the beauty of that flower that comes from the root of Jesse and gives light in the days of spring and by its fragrance has raised innumerable thousands from the dead. When he found an abundance of flowers, he preached to them and invited them to praise the Lord as though they were endowed with reason. In the same way he exhorted with the sincerest purity cornfields and vineyards, stones and forests and all the beautiful things of the fields, fountains of water and the green things of the gardens, earth and fire, air and wind, to love God and serve him willingly. Finally he called all creatures brother and sister, and in a most extraordinary manner, a manner never experienced by others, he discerned the hidden things of nature with his sensitive heart, as one who had already escaped into the freedom of the glory of the children of God. O good Jesus, he is now praising you as admirable in heaven with all the angels, he who on earth preached you as lovable to every creature. (Celano, XXIX, 72–73)

In every work of the artist he praised the Artist; whatever he found in the things made he referred to the Maker. He rejoiced in all the works of the hands of the Lord and saw behind things pleasant to behold their life-giving reason and cause. In beautiful things he saw Beauty itself; all things were to him good. "He who made us is the best," they cried out to him. Through his footprints impressed upon things he followed the

Beloved everywhere; he made for himself from all things a
ladder by which to come even to his throne . . . For that orig-
inal goodness that will be one day all things in all already
shown forth in this saint all things in all. (Celano, CXXIV,
269–270)

In contrast to Francis' deep understanding of the divine presence in nature, we have become a people who, having lost the
sense of the divine presence, are intent on destroying nature.

The painful wounds inflicted on creation by human hands
have led us into a deepening ecological crisis on a planetary
scale that we now know will lead to irreversible catastrophe for
all life, including the human race, if major changes are not initiated in the immediate decades ahead. Finding ourselves in this
profound ecological crisis forces the faith community to be critical of our theological tradition and practice. We must ask ourselves how the worldview of the church contributed to the
deepening crisis in the ecosystem. The current ecological crisis
is a theological crisis for us: as the church, we must wrestle with
the painful reality that our theology, worship, and ministry not
only have failed to defend creation but have contributed to its
exploitation and destruction.

To open this reflection, we need to let go of sentimental
notions of a Francis associated with birdbaths and assorted back-
yard statuary. We must begin to claim a relationship with him
as a guide, as a spiritual companion, and as the patron saint of
the environment. What clues do we have from the life of St.
Francis about the right relationship between human beings and
the rest of God's creation? A uniquely Franciscan vision of a
transformed relationship with creation is found in the Canticle
of Creation, written by Francis.

> Most High, all-powerful, all good Lord!
> All praise is yours, all glory, all honor and blessing.
> To You alone, Most High, do they belong.
> All praise be yours, my Lord, through all that you
>   have made,

And first my Lord, Brother Sun,
Who brings the day, and light You give us through
    him.
How beautiful is he, how radiant in all his splendor!
Of You, Most High, he bears the likeness.

All praise be yours, my Lord, through Sister Moon
    and Stars;
In the heavens you have made them bright and fair.

All praise be yours, my Lord, through Brothers Wind
    and Air,
And fair and stormy, all the weather's moods,
By which you cherish all that You have made.

All praise be yours, my Lord, through Sister Water,
So useful, lowly, precious and pure.

All praise be Yours, my Lord, through Brother Fire,
Through whom you brighten up the night.
How beautiful he is, how gay! Full of power and
    strength.

All praise be yours, my Lord, through Sister Earth,
    our mother,
Who feeds us in her sovereignty and produces
Various fruits and colored flowers and herbs.

All praise be yours, my Lord, through those who
    grant pardon
For love of You; through those who endure sickness
    and trial.
Happy those who endure in peace,
By you, Most High, they will be crowned.

All praise be yours, my Lord, through Sister Death,
From whose embrace no mortal can escape.

Woe to those who die in mortal sin!
Happy those she finds doing your will!
The second death can do no harm to them.

Praise and bless my Lord, and give thanks.
Serve God with great humility.

In the Canticle of Creation, Francis calls out to all of creation as brother and sister revealing the core of the Franciscan world-view—that God is the source of all being. The Creator God is the Parent, both Mother and Father of all creatures, who are therefore brother and sister to one another. Because all of creation is a part of this divine family, everything created, animate and inanimate, deserves brotherly and sisterly love and respect. The divine image or spark, the *"imago Dei"* that exists in human creatures, exists in all creatures. This divine image exists even in the "cornfields and vineyards . . . stones and forests . . . beautiful things of the field . . . fountains of water."

Walking Humbly with God and Creation

Francis reveled in the glory of God in creation. He lived out of a sense of ecstatic union with God's presence in all things. Francis called out to all the world in warm greetings: Brother! Sister! The nature of this encounter could be described in the language of the Jewish theologian Martin Buber as an "I-Thou" encounter. Buber recognized that reality is fundamentally two kinds of relationships. The impersonal, subject-object, "I-It" relationship, extended to all so-called objects, and in actuality to most human beings; and the "I-Thou" relationship, experienced in moments that honor the sacredness of human identity and personal relationship. Francis extends this "I-Thou" relationship to all that is. He invites us to see with him that the true nature of reality is expressed in the "I-Thou" relationship between God the Creator and all of creation. God is the God of sky, land, water, and all life. Everything has a relationship with God. Seeing this, we are invited to greet with gratitude all things as exuding the goodness of God.

Francis' Canticle of Creation is not just nice poetry. It is a profound celebration of creation as it really is and is meant to be. The canticle names reality as constituted in the relationship of all things as brother and sister. The canticle invites us to understand our destiny in the created world as a very simple one, that of walking in paradise. Francis lived out of an essential vision of paradise, a vision of what is God's original design for creation and what will be again when Creator and creation are reconciled, when God becomes "all in all." As the New Creation comes into being, we must be as present as possible to its unfolding: we must look for its signs and wonders and hear its groaning. Francis did this; this above all else is what set him apart from others: within the world that is, he could see the wonder of the world to be. This is what Celano meant when he said that Francis had "already escaped into the freedom of the glory of the children of God." Francis was experiencing in an anticipatory way the future to which we are all called. Francis was present to this New Creation because of his own transformation. The spirit of the Canticle has the power to enkindle within us a new longing for paradise as the harmonious communion of all creatures. We join Francis in the hope that the communion and relatedness of all in the primordial paradise shall exist again when history's struggle is resolved in that eschatological moment when all is made new.

In Francis of Assisi we have a companion and guide who teaches us to walk on the face of the earth with humility and with an open and grateful heart, aware of the divine goodness in all things. To do this, we must first let go of a self-understanding that is profoundly grandiose. To know our place on the earth is to respect boundaries and limits that have been set for us. When we think of ourselves as over and above creation, when we think of the world as a collection of "its" put there for us to exploit, we are participating in a worldview that allows, rationalizes, even encourages the exploitation of nature. To recover an ecological humility, we both affirm our worth as individuals and as a species and, at the same time, acknowledge our relative insignificance in the face of the cosmos. This new humility is historically analogous to the moment when Copernicus said to church and European society that the earth was not the center of the universe.

Once again, we are being called to accept a place for ourselves in creation that, however special, is not central. We as human creatures must dethrone ourselves as rulers of the universe. Only with this humility, this proper sense of self, can we recognize the intricate web of life on which we, with all other creatures, depend. Then we are able to begin to address every other creature as Sister and Brother, deserving of respect, compassion, and reverence. The witness of Francis calls us to "repent" of the pride that leads irresistibly to domination and alienation. With Franciscan humility, we can move in repentance from greed to thanksgiving and from exploitation to trust. We can recover a sense of the sacredness of life and place and matter. As we give thanks for all good things as coming from the hand of God, we recognize that the blessings of creation are intended for all, human and nonhuman.

Francis' example of reverence for the created order speaks to us today in ever new ways. With reason he is the patron of ecology, of those whose skill and calling it is to make the rest of us aware of earth's wonders and its fragility.

The gift of creation is also a call to responsibility. Created in the image of God, humanity's vocation is to participate fully with God in the process of creating a world where peace and justice reign, and to claim the divine image within us so that we can find our right relationship to creation. Much debate will continue in theological and ecological circles regarding humankind's role in relation to creation. To the "deep ecologist," the biblical concept of the stewardship of the earth is as much of a compromise as is the concept of domination, because it implies that we are unique as creatures, granted special freedoms and responsibilities to control and manipulate creation. For others, the idea of stewardship conveys the sense that we have been entrusted to be "gardeners" within the earth's garden — that we are called not to manipulate but to nourish and protect creation. Within every environmental position is the basic understanding that human beings possess the capacity for self-conscious reflection and moral awareness; we are capable of knowing the impact of our choices and of changing them. We must use this gift of consciousness well. We must continue to examine critically the theological imagery that we use to understand our relationship to the created order. This is an important and unfinished dialogue that is central to our mission to care for the earth and to do ecojustice. How we understand the divine image within is likely to determine how we do this work.

Scripture and Environmental Theology

The church's contribution to the ecological crisis began not from a lack of theological value and direction but from a misinterpretation of scripture. Scripture is a profound resource for the construction of an environmental theology and ministry. To initiate a rereading of our biblical tradition from the perspective of nature, we turn to Genesis. Our creation myth springs from the Hebrew affirmation of the earth as having a goodness given by the Creator. The story of the Garden of Eden is the story of an earthly paradise in which all creatures commune with one another and with the Creator in harmony. Adam and Eve are called to eat their fill and live in contentment and appreciation of the newly formed paradise. Their only task is one of naming, the act of defining and acknowledging that which has been created. God does not give to Adam and Eve the work of creating the other creatures, or even of controlling the environment of the garden.

Another understanding from the Hebrew Scriptures of our relationship to the land lies in Israel's belief that their God is revealed in the gift of a promised land. The God of Israel could be encountered in special, holy places, often on mountains. When Israel was conquered and carried off into exile, it was critical for the people to discover that in spite of the loss of their land, their God did not cease to exist; that their God is a universal God, faithful to them even in exile hundreds of miles from their homeland. The ancient Hebrew faith in a universal God never blinded the people to the God revealed in the particular patch of earth on which they stood.

Throughout the history of Israel, prophets were raised up to call the people back to a sense of the land as a divine gift by respecting the marginalized and poor, the widow and orphan, and the sojourner, who also have a right to reap the fruits of the land. The jubilee tradition challenged inequities in the ownership of the land by insuring that every fifty years the land would be redistributed among the people.

A strong theological basis for living respectfully with creation is also found in the New Testament; but here, too, our biblical tradition has been misinterpreted. The incarnation is a strong foundation for a theological affirmation of the goodness of creation. But the Western church, inheriting the dualistic worldviews of Greco-Roman culture, came to regard the material realm as inferior to the spiritual. This dualism not only contradicts the incarnation, it also contributes to a profound misunderstanding of the resurrection by making salvation synonymous with the ultimate fate of an immortal soul, which at the point of death abandons the physical world for the spiritual. The apostle Paul spoke of the resurrection of the body rather than the immortality of the soul because he affirmed, first, that body and soul are an indivisible unity and, second, that the reality of resurrection is a liberating process located not just in human identity but in the whole of creation. Through our bodies we are joined in solidarity with all of creation. The hope for the resurrection of the body, understood biblically, is the hope that all physical creation will be redeemed and transformed in the final triumph of divine love. It is the hope of a New Creation, fully established at the end of history when God will be "all in all" (1 Cor. 15:28). The struggles of the present, in which the Spirit groans with us and through us for freedom (Rom. 8:23), already anticipate this New Creation.

The Environment, Racism, and Economic Justice

The heart of our mission to create ecojustice lies in the equitable sharing of the goodness of creation. Creation is sufficient to meet the needs of all if her gifts are distributed justly. All humans can be fed, adequately sheltered, and given access to those resources necessary for the goodness of life without doing damage to the rest of creation. In fact, this is God's original intention for creation. Yet, this divine intention is too often thwarted. The "haves" of the first world have a disproportionate control over the resources of the earth, while those who work the land, the poor of the world, have little access to decision-making power and basic necessities, including land itself.

Herein we discover the indissoluble link between economic justice and the equitable distribution of the blessings of creation. Justice remains at the center of the environmental ethic. It is more and more urgent that citizens of the "first world" recognize the critical role that they must play in the just distribution of creation's blessings. We can no longer regard this role as one of charitable control; instead, we must recognize it as the way of relinquishment. We are called to relinquish our grasp on our excesses, so that others may have the basic necessities of life.

"First-world" citizens must be in dialogue with the poor and marginalized to hear clearly the cries of creation. For it is the poor who experience most directly creation's wounds. The environmental problems that afflict our society as a whole are often right on their doorstep. Three out of five Hispanic and African Americans live in communities with uncontrolled toxic waste dumps. The race and economic status of nearby residents are undeniably the leading factors in the location of commercial and hazardous waste facilities. It is only the poor and marginalized who can really teach our church and society about the critical link between justice and the environment. Communities of color are saying to the white environmental movement that a clean environment without social justice is environmental racism. White environmental activists desperately need to come to terms with this connection between racism, injustice, and environmental destruction. Here, too, the question of the divine image emerges: part of the environmental challenge is to recognize the divine image in all the peoples and cultures of the world.

As we seek to respond to this call of restoring the earth, we are called to see creation herself as the *anawim,* the biblical word for the ones whose voices are not heard. We are to be advocates for a wounded creation to those who cannot hear how creation is groaning and crying out to us.

Our God is being crucified once again in the environmental destruction of our time. We are called to accompany creation precisely at the point of her wounds, those places of brokenness and despoliation. The crucified God in solidarity with the brokenness of creation is also the God of resurrection, able to bring healing out of sickness, reconciliation out of alienation, and life out of death. To be faithful to the crucified and risen one present in creation, we must participate in this divine work of healing and reconciling creation.

The journey out of the environmental crisis will be a dangerous and consuming one. Francis gives us these gifts for the journey:

1) a vision of creation as a paradise in which every creature is sister and brother to us, a "Thou" deserving love and respect;

2) faith that God is also within us and that to recognize the divine image in humanity is humbly to accept our place in the created order that sustains all life;

3) a vocation grounded in the hope for a New Creation that God is bringing about in the celebration of life and in the struggle for justice on earth.

Vision, faith, and vocation: we are well equipped to accept the challenge of ecojustice and environmental stewardship. It is the call to paradise.

OUR STORIES

In the exercises to follow, you are invited to reflect on your encounters with creation at different points in your life.

• What was the geography of your childhood? Did you grow up in an urban, suburban, or rural setting? Did you play outdoors? Did you have any pets? Did you ever raise plants or crops? What are positive and negative memories of your childhood experience of nature? How do you think those circumstances shaped your view of nature? How have those childhood experiences of nature shaped your identity as an adult?

• Have you ever experienced what for you were moments of communion with nature when the distance between you and the rest of creation was bridged or overcome? Where and how did this happen? What did you feel? Did this experience change the way you view the world?

• Have you ever been confronted with the wounds inflicted on the natural world by humankind? Describe this encounter. What feelings did you have? Who or what was responsible for this wounding of the environment? What was your response to this situation?

SIGNS OF OUR TIMES

All Praise to You for Sister Water

Nearly two billion people have inadequate drinking water, and three billion lack proper sanitation. Because of this lack of sanitation, water-borne diseases cause an average of 25,000 deaths a day in the "two-thirds world." Eighty percent of child deaths in the "two-thirds world" are caused by human waste in water supplies.*

• What have been your attitudes and assumptions about the water available for your use? Consider how your socio-economic position in the United States or the position of the United States in the global community may have shaped your views about water resources. Consider what might be the point of view of a

---

*Information about water, air, and earth in the following sections is drawn from the United Nations Environmental Sabbath publication.

rural villager in Ghana who walks a mile to a creek to carry water back to her family's hut. How might her view differ from your own?

• What is the water situation in your community? Where does your water come from? Who really controls the water of your community? of the region in which you live? Which uses of water do you consider efficient, and which are wasteful? Does your community employ conservation of water? Do you? Who are the biggest polluters of water sources in your community or region? Who defines the criteria by which your community judges what is "acceptable" pollution in water sources?

All Praise to You for Brothers Wind and Air

Pollution in the atmosphere does not respect so-called national boundaries. Our global interdependence is brought home to us by the reality that we all breathe the same air. Some 20,000 lakes in Canada are now impaired by acid rain caused in large part by emissions from United States industry, power plants, and automobiles.

The depletion of the ozone layer is caused largely by industrial nations in the Northern hemisphere, and yet its effects are known in the South. As the ecological crisis grows, the relative size of the global community shrinks. Our planet has been encircled with a thin blanket of air that makes life possible. Yet in this generation, we proceed with the destruction of our atmosphere as if there were no consequences.

The United States accounts for around 25 percent of the carbon dioxide emissions in the earth's atmosphere. Most of this is from automobile exhaust. Reflect on the relationship between the U.S. auto industry and the average U.S. citizen who owns an automobile. In the therapeutic world, the concept of co-dependency has been introduced to describe how individuals sometimes cooperate with and even encourage destructive relationships or systems. Because they have found a way to have their interests met, the destructive relationship is preferred over less defined possibilities for healing and health. Using this concept of codependency, reflect on the reality of transportation and the habits, options, and choices that we make. What is the nature of our relationship with the automobile industry? What would a relationship of healthy interdependence look like?

All Praise to You for Sister Earth

If we view the earth as one organism, we can see that the rain forests across our planet are like the lungs of the body that cleanse the air we breathe. We are, in effect, destroying the earth's lungs by cutting down our rain forests at the rate of one football field per second. Each year tropical forests covering an area the equivalent of Austria are cut down. Tropical forests, which cover only 6 to 7 percent of the world's land area, contain over half the known plant and animal species, including 80 percent of insects and 90 percent of primates. The biodiversity of tropical forests is astounding. One of the world's five to ten million species becomes extinct every day. A million species may have vanished by the year 2000. The main cause of this process of extinction is the destruction of habitats, especially these biologically rich tropical forests being cleared for agricultural development, fuel wood, cattle grazing, and the lumber industry. Every Sunday, in the United States, more than 500,000 trees are used to produce the 88 percent of newspapers that are not recycled.

Recognizing the impact on the environment of such industries as lumber and cattle, reflect now on how these industries are connected to your own household and community. What connections do you see? In these relationships, do you perceive yourself as having power or lacking power?

INVITATION TO RESPOND

There is no global issue that is not first a local issue. It may be difficult at times to see how our actions can have an impact

FRANCIS AND CREATION   *119*

at the global level. It is easier to know what to do about our own neighborhood than about rain forests in the Amazon. But somehow we must continue to hold these struggles together. Global change is most likely to happen when each of us stands firmly rooted in our own reality and remembers our interconnectedness. The following action guidelines are offered to congregations and faith communities as possible steps for taking up or sustaining an environmental ministry. We recall how deeply grounded the early Franciscan community was to the places of San Damiano and La Portiuncula. The Franciscan community rebuilt those ruined churches as the material basis for their worship of God, their shared community, and their mission in the world. Congregations and faith communities are invited to explore their connections to land and to a sense of place.

Eco-theologian Geoffrey Lilburne has said that the foundation of an environmental ministry is in loving a given place—in seeking the well-being of that place and of all the creatures that it supports. The first step, says Lilburne, is to come to know the place where you stand. Define what area it is that you wish to come to know better. It may be the land upon which your church is built. It may be your neighborhood or local community. Identify sources of information that might help you understand the history of the land. Find out specifics around demographic patterns, the kinds of economic activity the land has sustained. See if there are elders in your community who can tell you stories about how the land once was. Are there other "historians" who can tell you who occupied the land before the Europeans? What can you find out about that people, their relationship to the land, and what happened to them? Bring together this story of the land upon which you stand. What do these facts and images relay to you about the land?

Reflect theologically on what shape the kingdom of God will take in this place.

• How does the Word of God take on the flesh of this piece of God's earth?

• What aspects of the ecojustice crisis particularly affect your community? Gather information on the needs of your community and then identify two regional or local ecological justice needs that deserve priority attention. Who are the principal victims, human and nonhuman, of ecological injustice so far? Who are likely to be next?

• What is being done by local voluntary organizations, interfaith groups, and government agencies to alleviate the crisis? How are people of color affected by these issues, and what is their response? What kind of environmental coalitions exist? Do they include people of color?

• How can you get more involved as individuals and as a community? Consider several ways to act: community education, service, use of investments, change in lifestyle, or public policy advocacy.

• Brainstorm a list of next steps that you can take as individuals and as a community. Affirm that common action is important, even though not everyone is ready for the same level of engagement. The object is not to make individuals feel guilty if they are not doing "enough," but for each person to feel empowered to do what he or she can — to take one step at a time. The crucial thing is to do one thing! Take the next step and trust that it will lead you forward.

(Adapted from *Keeping and Healing the Creation*, a resource paper by The Presbyterian Eco-Justice Task Force, issued by the Committee on Social Witness Policy, Presbyterian Church [U.S.A.], 1989.)

7

FRANCIS AND SUFFERING

Dialogue with the Crucified and Risen One

He called the crowd with his disciples, and said to them, "If any want to become my followers, let them deny themselves and take up their cross and follow me. For those who want to save their life will lose it, and those who lose their life for my sake, and for the sake of the gospel, will save it. For what will it profit them to gain the whole world and forfeit their life?" (Mark 8:34–36)

While we live we are constantly being delivered to death for Jesus' sake, so that the life of Jesus may be revealed in our mortal flesh. Death is at work in us, but life in you. (2 Cor. 4:11–12)

FRANCIS' STORY

In September of 1224, two years before his death, after a period of intense activity, Francis made a retreat at a place called Mt. Alverna. There on a rugged cliffside of this lonely mountain he entered into a forty-day period of fasting, solitude, and prayer. In this poverty, Francis received an inpouring of the Spirit such as he had never known before. As Francis read the gospel account of Christ's passion, he experienced an unquenchable desire to be with Christ in his suffering. As he continued in prayer, Francis realized that what he longed for was to be given to him in a very mysterious way. The following account describes the revelation that he received just before the wounds of Christ, the stigmata, appeared in his hands, feet, and side.

The next day came, that is, the Feast of the Cross. And St. Francis, sometime before dawn, began to pray outside the entrance of his cell, turning his face toward the east. And he prayed in this way:

"My Lord Jesus Christ, I pray you to grant me two graces before I die: the first is that during my life I may feel in my soul and in my body, as much as possible, that pain which You, dear Jesus, sustained in the hour of Your most bitter passion. The second is that I may feel in my heart, as much as possible, that excessive love with which You, O Son of God, were inflamed in willingly enduring such suffering for us sinners."

And remaining for a long time in that prayer, he understood that God would grant it to him, and that it would soon be conceded to him to feel those things as much as is possible for a mere creature.

Having received this promise, St. Francis began to contemplate with intense devotion the Passion of Christ and His infinite charity. And the fervor of his devotion increased so much within him that he utterly transformed himself into Jesus through love and compassion. And while he was thus inflaming himself in this contemplation, on that same morning he saw coming down from heaven a seraph with six resplendent and flaming wings. As the seraph, flying swiftly, came closer to St. Francis, so that he could perceive him clearly, he noticed that He had the likeness of a crucified man, and his wings were so disposed that two wings extended above His head, two were spread out to fly, and the other two covered his entire body.

On seeing this, St. Francis was very much afraid, and at the same time he was filled with joy and grief and amazement. He felt intense joy from the friendly look of Christ, who appeared to him in a very familiar way and gazed at him very kindly. But on the other hand, seeing Him nailed to the cross, he felt boundless grief and compassion. Next, he was greatly amazed at such an astounding and extraordinary vision, for he knew well that the affliction of suffering is not in accord with the immortality of the angelic seraph. And while he was marveling thus, He who was appearing to him revealed to him that this vision was shown to him by Divine Providence in this particular form in order that he should understand that he was to be utterly transformed into the direct likeness of Christ Crucified, not by physical martyrdom, but by enkindling of the mind. (Brown, 190–91)

Perhaps of all the stories of Francis that we have considered, it is the account of Francis on Mt. Alverna that is most difficult for our modern sensibilities. Any initial skepticism about the historicity of this story makes it easier for us to dismiss this as the stuff of medieval legend. And yet, it is hard for the most critical historian to dispute the testimony of friars who saw the wounds on Francis in spite of his efforts to conceal them. Do we not know from our own experience that the mind is intimately related to the body? Is it then impossible for an interior state, lived more and more intensely over a lifetime, to manifest itself in the exterior body?

It is not the intention here to convince anyone of the historicity of the stigmata. Everyone must interpret the truth of this story for him- or herself. Our real problem may come at another level, when we are tempted to dismiss the story of the stigmata as just another example of medieval asceticism and piety that we find unhealthy and grossly negative. Doesn't this story of the stigmata of Francis glorify suffering in a way that seems inappropriate to us today?

The modern religious attitude toward suffering is fundamentally different from that in the time of Francis. Suffering is not understood as necessary for salvation or as deserved because of original sin. Furthermore, so much suffering in the world neither ennobles those who suffer, nor contributes anything positive to their existence. But with all these theological and ethical reservations aside, how do we come to terms with suffering in our lives and in our world? More specifically, what is the relationship between our faith and the suffering that we feel and see all around us? Does Francis have anything to teach us about a faithful and transforming response to suffering?

Before we return to the story of Francis on Mt. Alverna, let us look at his response to suffering over the context of a lifetime. In what ways did Francis know suffering? What consequences did it have for him? What meaning was he able to draw from these experiences? What can we learn from the ways in which suffering was present in the life of Francis and how he responded to it?

Suffering and the Conversion of Francis

As a young man in the prime of his life, Francis experienced first-hand the shattering realities of warfare, imprisonment, and debilitating sickness. These experiences undoubtedly contributed to the profound crisis in his life that led to his conversion. Through these very painful experiences, the world of Francis was "cracked open" and his ego broken, so that something new could be born.

As we considered in chapter 1, the movement of his conversion carried Francis from the point of finding the suffering of a leper utterly repulsive to the point at which he could embrace the leper as a brother or sister and offer him or her care and support. Francis no longer feared but embraced the physical and emotional suffering of the most marginalized of his society. His experience of the world was enlarged to include that which had formerly been rejected and shunned. And in the context of this new enlarged worldview, the suffering leper was no longer repulsive but "sweet" to his inner heart. Clearly, a transformation had begun to occur. Francis teaches us that human suffering may be the occasion for a transforming moment of conversion. Experiences of suffering have the potential to open us to a new understanding of ourselves and God. Suffering can sensitize us to the pain of the world. Our experiences of suffering can link us to larger communities of suffering and support of which we have been largely unaware, energizing us for struggle and advocacy on fronts that have become very personal.

The painful alienation that Francis felt in relation to his family and especially his father grew until these relationships reached a breaking point in that dramatic moment in the cathedral courtyard of Assisi. When Francis stood naked before the bishop, his family, and all of the townspeople, he removed himself from the security of family and community. Jesus taught this same lesson in a number of those "hard sayings" directed at those who would follow him (e.g., "Leave father and mother behind," "Let the dead bury the dead"). He experienced painful rejection from his home town when he returned to preach in the synagogue of Nazareth. How many of us have known painful alienation from our family of origin or our home town or ethnic community because we have sought to be faithful to a different path?

In chapter 2, we considered how Francis relinquished any claim to protection and status, shelter and livelihood that his family could provide him. Francis moved from his former life at the center of a walled city to a life outside the walls, vulnerable to the painful inequities of the poorest of the poor. For Francis and for Clare the invitation to discipleship meant the willingness to risk alienation from one's community. It meant the willingness to make oneself insecure and vulnerable to suffering. The call to conversion meant fundamentally a willingness to relinquish all claims on one's former life.

Francis and his brothers and sisters willingly and joyfully embraced the physical hardship and suffering that the poor of that time experienced involuntarily at the margins of social existence. Fundamental to their mission in the world as followers of Christ was this compassionate solidarity with the marginalized. Wearing only coarse tunics on their backs and living most of the time in what amounted to lean-tos made of sticks and brush, Francis and his brothers knew the discomforts of nature as the most marginalized in his society must have known them. They knew the hardships of inadequate shelter that barely shielded them from the cold of winter or the heat of summer. They knew the back-breaking labor of the peasant working the fields. They knew the gnawing emptiness of hunger of those who eked out an existence from day to day. This was a conscious choice, an intentional pastoral strategy that was radically rooted in the witness of the historical Jesus and in the discipleship journey that ends and begins anew at the foot of the cross. They bore in their bodies and souls the suffering of the poor, believing that they were bearing the suffering Christ.

But the original Franciscan community was not a collection of individuals all demonstrating tremendous feats of ascetic self-denial. Rather, it was a community seeking to be faithful to a call to live on the margins and intent on helping one another to be faithful to that difficult mission. This may be the most important aspect of the Franciscan witness of suffering.

Francis himself was not an ascetic superhuman able to endure all suffering by the sheer force of his spirituality. It was his friend and sister Clare who so often sustained him through the most difficult and painful moments of his life. Their intimacy and constant love for each other enabled Francis to endure extremely difficult crises of vision and leadership within the order. In those years when his health began to fail him, Francis sought out the company and solace of Clare who nurtured him through the physical agonies of the last year before his death.

This deep tenderness in the relationship between Francis and Clare characterized the quality of life of the Franciscan community in the relations of all the brothers and sisters. Their community was one in which each bore the other's burdens; a community that ministered to one another in sickness, trial, and want.

Francis and Bodily Suffering

Toward the end of his life, Francis was racked with pain from a very serious eye disease that threatened his sight and made ordinary sunlight an unbearable torment. On one occasion, his brothers finally persuaded him to avail himself of the best medical remedies available to him in that day. Unfortunately, medical opinion was that cauterization of the temples would relieve the agonizing pain that Francis experienced in his eyes. As the doctor prepared the hot iron to cauterize his temples in what would be an excruciating procedure, Francis pleaded with Brother Fire to be gentle with him. And it is reported by witnesses and by Francis himself that when the operation was performed, he felt no pain. Francis was one who could dialogue with his pain, talking to it not as an enemy but as if it were a brother or sister.

When his deteriorating health finally brought Francis to the point of death, he composed the last stanza of the Canticle:

> All praise be yours, my Lord, through Sister Death,
>   from whose embrace no mortal can escape.

From these lines, sung by the brothers in those last hours, we see that Francis was able to greet and welcome even death as a sister. He embraced the end of his life as something to be celebrated rather than feared. Elias, the friar who would replace Francis as the leader of the order, rebuked Francis at the hour of his death for singing rather than saying prayers of confession and mourning. But Francis kept on singing for joy. As death drew near, Francis requested that the brothers lay him naked on the ground, in imitation of Christ and in his desire to be close to the earth. For Francis, even death was a joyous occasion.

Francis and the Suffering of the Cross

The life of St. Francis has much to teach us about how to integrate the suffering that comes to us as fragile creatures. Like any human being, Francis knew the pain resulting from conflict and injustice, sickness, accident, aging, and death. But the suffering that Francis knew on Mt. Alverna transcends these experiences of suffering because it was born of a conscious choice to embrace with his whole being the suffering and the love of the crucified Christ. The gift of the stigmata was not simply a miracle given near the end of Francis' life. It was rather the fruit of his whole faith journey, the culminating moment of an entire life-time of striving to identify more and more with the crucified Christ. Francis sought to make his very existence cruciform, by drawing more and more of his life and experience into the reality of the cross. It was finally on Mt. Alverna that this intention manifested itself physically in his body in the wounds of the crucified Christ.

We reflect again on the prayer that shaped Francis' experience on Mt. Alverna:

> *My Lord Jesus Christ, I pray you to grant me two graces before I die: the first is that during my life I may feel in my soul and in my body, as much as possible, that pain which You, dear Jesus, sustained in the hour of Your most bitter passion. The second is that I may feel in my heart as much as possible, that excessive love with which You, O Son of God, were inflamed in willingly enduring such suffering for us sinners.*

On Mt. Alverna, Francis prayed that his heart might be opened to compassionate solidarity so that he could feel the suffering of Christ on the cross as well as the love that motivated Christ to endure that pain.

At the core of Franciscan spirituality is this striving to enter into the divine heart to feel the pathos of suffering love that God feels for the world. Francis' striving to identify with the crucified Christ was not meant to be a spiritual absorption into suffering for its own sake and should not be construed as a masochistic sanctification of pain. Rather, Francis sought to know God by abiding with God in the passion. Francis embodied and illuminates the words of St. Paul when he wrote of "filling up in ourselves what is lacking in the sufferings of Christ." Francis believed that if we claim to be the body of Christ, we are called to participate in the suffering, death, and resurrection of Jesus. We are called to die and be raised again in new life, not just at the end of our life but in each moment of our discipleship journey. Francis accompanies us in following Jesus in the way of the cross, the way of active love on behalf of the crucified of the world.

The Scandal of the Cross

Francis points beyond himself to the gospel story and asks us our response to the cross of Christ. Here we reach a fundamental problem: the scandal of the crucified God. Jesus died in what seemed to be a complete rupture from his own mission, from his community, and ultimately from his God. Jesus, the one who proclaimed the nearness of God the Father, was hung on the cross seemingly abandoned by God. The gospel message of the cross is a scandal and stumbling block because it does not bring us the message of success or the triumphant power of goodness, but of God's presence hidden in what is defeat, loss, abandonment, and death. How is it that the divine being is revealed in the agony of a crucifixion?

As the original discipleship community experienced a profound crisis in the loss of their leader and in the manner of his death, so the first generations of the church were faced with the difficulty of interpreting to the world they sought to evangelize how the death of Jesus could mean anything other than the disastrous end of an obscure messianic movement in a remote corner of the Roman empire. In just what sense was there "good news" to be found in the death of one denounced as a blasphemer by the religious establishment of his society and executed as a political revolutionary by the imperial power of the Roman state?

The church was tempted to resolve this problem by removing the scandal of the cross. We see this "temptation" reflected in the gospel accounts themselves. As Mark is considered the most original, its perspective on the crucifixion is the most stark. Mark's Jesus cries out from the cross, " My God, my God, why hast thou forsaken me?" For Mark, the way of the cross, the way of solidarity and resistance, is the historical paradigm for the discipleship journey, the path that any disciple of Jesus must be prepared to follow. Luke's account, much later than Mark's, tones down the death of Jesus by transforming the crucified one into a confident martyr, who is obedient to divine necessity. And in the Gospel of John, Jesus becomes the exalted one orchestrating the final events of his earthly life before he ascends into heaven.

Throughout the history of the church, this temptation to remove the historical scandal of the crucifixion has resulted in theologies of the cross that provide doctrinal explanations of why the cross had to be and why it makes perfect sense. The cross has been interpreted solely as a symbol of divine forgiveness for the individual rather than as the cost of discipleship. The church has softened the scandal by separating the cross of Jesus from the historical path that led to it. The historical path of the cross led Jesus to the margins of his society in loving solidarity with the outcast and into an ever deepening conflict with the authorities for their maintenance of systems that exclude and dominate. This path would ultimately lead Jesus through the dark night of betrayal and desertion, through trial, torture, and execution.

We must not give in to this temptation to remove the scandal of the cross of Jesus. The cross is not meant to provide neat answers to our inquiry about the nature of God, nor does it provide easy images of divine wisdom. Rather, the cross reveals the inadequacy of human knowledge to comprehend the ways of God. The cross challenges the assumption that human knowledge is able to understand God at all. And so the cross is scandal and folly to human reason. In the same way, the cross directly challenges human strength and power. Far from revealing an omnipotent God wielding power from heaven, the cross reveals a God hidden in the profoundly negative depths of history, the garbage dump called Golgotha. God is revealed in weakness rather than strength, in failure rather than success.

The cross radically undercuts the standards of the world, exposing how the divine gifts of human power and intelligence are easily coopted by evil and for the purposes of oppression. The cross is a challenge that goes to the very foundation of human reason and power by asking, "Are human reason and power the instruments of oppression and violence or of justice and liberation?" The cross of Jesus exposes human reason and power as false gods, whenever they claim for themselves an absolute authority. Any time that human power or reason are used to carry out or justify oppression, these human potentialities declare themselves to be in open rebellion against the Reign of God.

The message of the gospel was a scandal to the Jews and a stumbling block to the Greeks because of the claim that God is revealed in the form of one hanging from a cross. The gospel message says that on the cross God is crucified. This message continues to be, in every generation, the foolishness of God in the face of human reason, and the weakness of God in the face of human power. The cross is folly and continues to be a stumbling block when it is not glossed over into a more palatable religious symbol. And so we ask ourselves again: What meaning do we find in this event of the cross, the death of Jesus? In what sense does God suffer for us and for our world in the crucifixion of Jesus of Nazareth?

The Scandal of the World's Suffering

If we are able to view the cross of Jesus without removing the scandal of the crucifixion, we are more likely to face without rationalization or denial the scandal of the world's suffering. Any theology of the cross that does not help us to see and address this scandal is irrelevant and inappropriate. An authentic theology of the cross must enable us to face the scandal of the unspeakable suffering of millions, in fact the vast majority of the human race who are afflicted with violence and marginalized by poverty and injustice. And so it is the scandal of the cross borne by the vast majority of the world that provides an urgent context for our reflection as we ask the question: What does the cross say to the suffering of those who are oppressed, hungry, homeless, and abandoned?

This question is best answered by those who actually suffer, especially by the faithful who occupy the margins of society. The authors of this book have had the privilege of being with the peoples of Latin America in countries like Nicaragua, El Salvador, Honduras, Guatemala, Peru, and Bolivia. The suffering of the people in these countries has been bitter, longstanding, and immense. For millions of faceless and nameless souls throughout Latin America, the experience of suffering has been an excruciating barrier to a humane existence. There is no way to say that this suffering has somehow ennobled or purified the poor of Latin America. We must resist the temptation to remove the scandal and offense of this suffering with any romantic distortion. This suffering is an abomination and an absolute contradiction to the will of God.

But in the midst of this history of suffering, there have been communities of faith in Latin America and elsewhere that have been able to approach the mystery and the scandal of the cross with an intuitive understanding rooted in their own context and struggle. In Christ crucified they have seen the God who is in complete and absolute solidarity with all the crucified of the world. This divine love embraces the crucified ones of the world in order to transform their condition: to alleviate their pain, to heal their wounds, to walk with them in the struggle to transform situations of injustice and oppression. The God revealed in Jesus does not go about this liberating work from afar, but from within history, in the very midst of death, even from the cross. As long as anyone continues to suffer, God continues to suffer on the cross.

The message of the cross has the power to save, to renew the people of Latin America with courage and hope because they know in their hearts that God is with them in their struggle for life. With the assurance that their pain is God's pain, they work and hope for a future free of suffering. The faith of the poor in the crucified is also a faith in the risen one who is even now alive and accompanies the people, not yet in final triumph, but hidden in history's struggle, yearning for history's liberation. If it seems that in the "first-world" church we often skip over the cross altogether as a transition on the way to the resurrection, the church of the "third world," especially in Latin America, may appear to proclaim a gospel dominated by the cross and devoid of the promise of the resurrection. But this is not so. People of faith in Latin America experience in their own lives this constant dialectic between the cross of Jesus and the resurrection of Christ. Their faith in the crucified is not separate from their faith in the risen one.

They lay claim to the power of the resurrection by their faith that they are accompanied by the crucified one. This faith is strengthened by the witness of their martyrs who, having suffered and died in the struggle for justice, are resurrected in the hope and life of the people.

Discipleship Journey Is the Way of the Cross

Out of this history of suffering, there have been these faithful communities who, out of a deep awareness of being accompanied by the God of love, have been able to rise up, shoulder their own crosses, and follow Jesus in the way of his passion. As people of faith in and outside the "Third World" have taken action to resist evil and the causes of suffering, they begin to enter ever more deeply into the reality of the cross. Such Christians stand in a long minority tradition in the history of the church, a tradition of fools like Francis whose passionate identification with the crucified Christ has led them into radical commitments on behalf of a suffering world.

In Jesus, Peter, and Paul, in Dietrich Bonhoeffer, Oscar Romero, Dorothy Kazel, Maura Clark, Jean Donovan, and Ita Ford, and in countless others, we honor this long tradition of prophets who endured suffering in order to speak the truth, who proclaimed hope in the inbreaking of justice and peace in the midst of injustice and conflict. We honor these "fools" who have defended life and who refused to be chased away by forces that threatened them with death, these "fools" who followed Jesus in the "*via negativa*," the way of the cross.

The call to take up the cross of Christ is the invitation to be in solidarity with the crucified of the world and to die with Christ in order to bring about the New Creation. The cross confronts us with the question of our own willingness to enter more deeply into union with God's suffering love for a broken world. We are called to embrace the struggle of the crucified of the world, to suffer if need be in solidarity with and alongside the poor and the marginalized. The followers of Jesus can expect persecutions precisely because of our resistance to those conditions which violate human dignity.

This invitation is as difficult to respond to now as it has always been. In every generation, the response entails contradicting enormous religious, political, economic, and social forces. Today, it means embracing the marginalized in compassionate solidarity as one's brother or sister, and resisting with all one's being the causes of their suffering. Compassionate solidarity means struggling against "powers and principalities," political and economic systems that shape the world and cause the suffering of millions of our brothers and sisters. Compassionate solidarity means struggling to re-create the systems that bring harm and pain and change them into systems that can mediate justice and community.

Do we not fear for the soul of the church in the "first world," when something so central to the gospel message, "Take up your cross and follow me," is so little practiced? When the "first-world" church contemplates the cross, for the most part it sees only an innocuous icon totally divorced from the painful historical reality. We have effectively eliminated the scandal of the cross by separating the cross of Jesus from the historical path that led to it, the path we are called to follow as disciples of Christ. We have sought to circumvent the cross and go directly to the "good news" of the resurrection. We have sought out a religious faith that eliminates the costs of discipleship and numbs us to the suffering of the world. If we cannot face the scandal of the cross of Jesus, we will not be able to face the scandal of the unjust suffering of millions in human history and in our world today.

If we were to truly open our eyes and to "see with eyes that see," we would no longer be able to avoid the great ocean of human suffering throughout history up to our own time. The human soul understandably recoils from such a horrible vision of pain. This vision strikes us in the core of our being and in deep places of personal pain. We shrink back in ignorance because the mind cannot grasp; in indifference because the will cannot respond; in numbness because the emotions collapse. If I truly open my life and my heart to the suffering of God in the world, will I not be immediately paralyzed, overwhelmed by the immensity of it? What kind of spirituality will make it possible to open ourselves to the divine heart and to abide with God in suffering love for the world?

A Spirituality of the Cross

A spirituality of the cross begins to emerge wherever people of faith become aware that "nothing can separate us from the love of God." A loving God is present in the midst of our suffering. But a spirituality based on the cross means far more than the acceptance of sadness and life's inevitable hardships.

A spirituality based on the cross must ultimately mean following the historical path that for Jesus led to the cross. In following Jesus, we bear the cross in our resistance to sin, both personal and collective. We bear the cross in our willingness to confront the idolatrous claims sometimes made by human reason and power. We proclaim what is foolishness in the face of human ideology. We proclaim what is weakness in the face of human power and the will to oppress.

True identification with the crucified one as experienced by Francis will not take place in the abstract as a religious ideal or by way of good intentions. This identification with the crucified one is authentically realized by following Jesus' way of the cross. But this gospel invitation does not demand directly that we suffer; rather, it calls us to love, which, because of evil, will mean suffering.

Here it is important to return to Mt. Alverna, where Francis sought to know God by abiding with Jesus in his passion. Had the revelation on Mt. Alverna been an isolated event, divorced from the context of Francis' life, its witness for us would be suspect and severely limited. The giving of the stigmata would be only a mystical glorification of suffering. But from Mt. Alverna, we can look back with Francis over his entire lifetime to see the path of discipleship that he sought to follow. In this way, we understand that a truly Franciscan spirituality is not so much a mysticism of suffering as it is a spirituality of following Jesus. Francis teaches us how we can take up our own cross and walk the path of our discipleship journey. He teaches us that the way of the cross is a never-ending process of conversion, of dying and rising to new life. We must find ways to deepen this conversion of "eyes, ears, and heart" so that we are able to recognize the crucified Christ in the face of the leper.

We must find ways to dispel the psychic numbness that stifles our compassion and to unlock the untapped capacity for love in our hearts. In faithful community we can gather the courage needed to face conflicts with our families and our society when the call to discipleship leads us along a different path. In community we receive and give the support that is necessary if we are to be faithful to our mission.

With each step along this path and with Francis as our companion we find ourselves more willing to relinquish the absolute claim on our lives and increasingly able to let go of those things that may insulate us from the suffering of the world. We walk with Francis step by difficult step toward the margins where we encounter and enter places of suffering. There we may experience many emotions: fear, revulsion, hurt, anger, love. Our fear gradually decreases as we learn to dialogue with those who suffer and with our own pain; we learn again how to care for others and how to be cared for; we begin to learn what it means to accompany someone in his or her struggle and to be accompanied in ours. We find that we are more willing to risk ourselves not out of self-destructiveness but because of our compassionate identification with others who suffer.

As we probe the deeper causes of unjust suffering in our world, we take up the struggle against mammoth structures that inflict suffering. We do this with a hope that is not rooted in our own efforts or dependent on the expectation of success. We confront radical evil as if our efforts could make a difference. Here the grace of the stigmata may be given to faithful individuals and communities who are seeking to enter more deeply into the pain of the world. These individuals and communities bear in their lives the wounds of Christ as they are asked to suffer with the people. Our mutual solidarity with others begins to teach us about the oneness of the human family, indeed the oneness of creation. From Mt. Alverna we hear the cries of all creation expressed in that cry of one hanging from the cross. And we know that we are not alone. We know that our suffering is God's, and that nothing in life or in death can separate us from the love of God.

From Mt. Alverna we stand with Francis in contemplation of the cross of compassionate solidarity. We pray that our hearts will be filled with the love for which Christ died on the cross for the people of God, for it is to this death that we are called, to die and be raised new women and men who struggle and hope for a new world. From Mt. Alverna we see with Francis the vision of a time when the scandalous suffering of the people, indeed the suffering of all creation, will be embraced in healing love and death will be overthrown, encompassed by transforming life. From Mt. Alverna we recognize that mysterious joining of suffering and joy in the compassionate heart that cannot be analyzed or even adequately described. We catch a glimpse of this grace in the life of Francis. The presence of joy in the midst of struggle and suffering is the most mature fruit of the Christian life, a sure sign of the working of the Spirit. This joy is also a seed of promise that points toward the glorious future to which we are all called, when God will be all in all.

We began this reflection with a story of Francis on Mt. Alverna; we close with the story of a Franciscan in the twentieth century who in April 1945 was one of several thousand captives jammed into a freight train moving through Germany. As the allied armies penetrated deeper and deeper into Germany, the Nazi SS herded the survivors of the concentration camp Buchenwald onto a train headed for some unknown place. Among these wretched souls from all social classes and nationalities was a small band of Franciscans. For endless days those passengers on this death train descended into a hell of torment as they experienced the suffering of hunger, exposure, violence, and radical evil. One Franciscan wrote of that experience:

> These extremities of suffering plunge us into acute anxiety. It is no longer simply the anxiety that grips any living thing as death approaches. Amid our terrible distress there arises in us a strange feeling that eats away at those inmost certainties which till now had sustained us. We have a growing impression that we have been handed over to some blind, savage power. There we are, thousands of men abandoned to hunger, cold, vermin, and death. The human being is completely crushed. [The human] whom we had till now believed was made in God's image, now seems laughable: worthless, helpless, hopeless; a being caught up in a whirlwind of forces that play with him, or rather, pay absolutely no attention to him. That is how we see ourselves now—that, and nothing more.
>
> Among the corpses that lie in the water of the car, eyes turned back, is a companion or a friend. Everything we can see, every experience we must undergo, tells us we are in the grip of an iron law, handed over to the play of blind forces—and that this, and this alone, is reality.
>
> Black night fills our souls. And yet, on the morning of April 26 when one of us is in his last moments and the light has almost left his eyes, what rises from our hearts to our lips is not a cry of despair or rebellion, but a song, a song of praise: Francis of Assisi's Canticle of Brother Sun! Nor do we have to force ourselves to sing it. It rises spontaneously out of our darkness and nakedness, as though it were the only language fit for such a moment. What brings us in such circumstances to praise God for and through the great cosmic brotherhood? Theories have no place in our utter confusion of spirit; they offer no shelter against the storm. The only thing that remains and is priceless in our eyes is the patience and friendship this or that comrade

shows you. Such an act by someone who, like yourself, is immersed in suffering and anxiety, is a ray of light that falls miraculously into the wretched darkness that envelops us. It re-creates you, makes you a human being once again. (Leclerc, 233-34)

OUR STORIES

Reflect on times or places of pain in your life.

• Did anyone accompany you through this time? Have you come to know yourself in a different way through these times of suffering? Have you come to know God in a new way? Was that time of suffering in your life ultimately humanizing or dehumanizing? Did that experience of suffering introduce you into a larger community of suffering that you had been unaware of prior to your own experience?

• Describe a time in which you encountered the suffering of another. What was the nature of that suffering and how did it affect you? Did it open emotional space within you or close you down? What was your response, and why do you think you responded in that way?

• What has your family or faith community taught you about the way to deal with suffering in your life? in the world? How has your understanding of suffering evolved through your life experience? Does your faith shape your response to the experience of suffering?

• Have you ever experienced rejection or revilement for a condition over which you had no control? How did you respond to this? What effects did it have on you?

• Have you ever suffered pain for a decision that you made on moral grounds? What did that feel like to you? How did you respond?

SIGNS OF OUR TIMES/INVITATION TO RESPOND

It is difficult to know for sure in what sense Francis may have tried to move beyond compassion to changing the social structures and systems that create suffering. The one who preached a sermon simply by walking silently through the streets of Assisi undoubtedly understood that actions proclaim a message. His life at the margins was in itself a prophetic witness. Like Jesus, Francis made a political statement by locating himself with the poor and marginalized.

The question is one of the church's own self-image as it ministers to the world. For so many generations, we have understood our mission in the world as charity to the poor. We have analyzed the problem of the suffering of the poor as something that we, the "haves," can ameliorate by generous redistribution of resources. As we begin to regard our faith in a more global context, we come to a much more profound understanding of the sources of the suffering of the poor. Aware as no other generation before us, we see on the nightly news and in the morning newspaper the suffering sea of humanity across the world. And we are coming to understand that all the people of the earth share an interdependent web of economic resources and political relationships.

The following reflection helps us to look at how we move from solidarity with the marginalized to confrontation with systems.

Let us revisit the parable of the good Samaritan, which has become for many in the church a very important ethical foundation for social action. The hero finds someone bloodied and beaten, lying in a ditch, near death. Unlike others who pass by the victim unmoved, the good Samaritan responds with compassion by taking the victim to an inn and paying for his medical care and upkeep. If on his next trip the Samaritan were to encounter yet another person in the ditch, we could hope that his compassionate response would be the same. But how many times would this happen before the Samaritan began to ask why this was happening. Perhaps he would realize that the truly compassionate act is to find out what situations are creating so many victims.

His compassion would take the form of an inquiry. "Why are there bandits along this road? How can they be stopped from this violence? What can be done to give the bandits themselves alternatives to violence?" The good Samaritan would be, in fact, engaging in a form of social analysis.

This is the challenge to compassionate people everywhere as we encounter in the ditch the victims of society. There is an obvious urgency to respond to the immediate needs of the person lying in the ditch. But eventually, if our compassion is to be effective, we must ask ourselves the question, "Why?" Why is this happening? What are the conditions that create victims? What are the political, economic, and cultural systems that define and affect this situation of suffering?

Reflect on one experience of suffering that you have encountered. This experience of suffering has had an impact on your life or on persons for whom you care. It has also been brought about by recognizably social causes. Let your compassion for the concrete person in the ditch take the shape of an inquiry as you probe to find out how and why this suffering happens and who may benefit from it. Who are the losers in this situation? Are there winners? Look behind the immediate circumstances of the victim and his or her suffering and consider the larger political and economic and cultural conditions that shape this experience. Analyze which systems contribute to this suffering and which minimize it. What kinds of systemic change are needed to alleviate this suffering? Allow your compassion and your anger to reenter the situation and move you to respond.

8

Francis and Contemplation

Dialogue with the Spirit

Shadrach, Meshach, and Abednego, servants of God thrown into a fiery furnace by Babylonian king Nebuchadnezzar, began to sing:

> Bless the Lord, all you works of the Lord ...
> Angels of the Lord, bless the Lord ...
> You heavens, bless the Lord ...
> All you waters above the heavens, bless the Lord ...
> All you hosts of the Lord, bless the Lord ...
> Sun and moon, bless the Lord ...
> Stars of heaven, bless the Lord ...
> Every shower and dew, bless the Lord ...
> All you winds, bless the Lord ...
> Fire and heat, bless the Lord ...
> [Cold and chill, bless the Lord ...
> Dew and rain, bless the Lord ...]
> Frost and chill, bless the Lord ...
> Ice and snow, bless the Lord ...
> Nights and days, bless the Lord ...
> Light and darkness, bless the Lord ...
> Lightnings and clouds, bless the Lord ...
> Let the earth bless the Lord ...
> Mountains and hills, bless the Lord ...
> Everything growing from the earth, bless the
>   Lord ...

You springs, bless the Lord . . .
Seas and rivers, bless the Lord . . .
You dolphins and all water creatures . . .
All you birds of the air, bless the Lord . . .
All you beasts, wild and tame, bless the Lord . . .
(Dan. 3:57–81)

This hymn of all creatures to their Creator was sung morning after morning throughout the years by Francis, alone or with the brothers.

These are the very things that God has revealed to us through the Spirit, for the Spirit reaches the depths of everything, even the depths of God . . . Now instead of the spirit of the world we have received the Spirit that comes from God, to teach us to understand the gifts that [God] has given us. (1 Cor. 2:10, 12)

FRANCIS' STORY

Sometimes Francis would act in the following way. When the sweetest melody of spirit would bubble up in him, he would give exterior expression to it in French, and breath of the divine whisper which his ear perceived in secret would burst forth in French in a song of joy. At times, as we saw with our own eyes, he would pick up a stick from the ground and putting it over his left arm, would draw across it, as across a violin, a little bow bent by means of a string; and going through the motions of playing, he would sing in French about his Lord. This whole ecstasy of joy would be dissolved in compassion for the passion of Christ. Then this saint would bring forth continual sighs, and amid deep groanings, he would be raised up to heaven, forgetful of the lower things he held in his hand. (Celano, XL, 242)

St. Francis maintained that the safest remedy against the thousand snares and wiles of the enemy is spiritual joy. For he

would say: "Then the devil rejoices most when he can snatch away spiritual joy from a servant of God. He carries dust so that he can throw it into even the tiniest chinks of conscience and soil the candor of mind and purity of life. But when spiritual joy fills hearts," he said, "the serpent throws off his deadly poison in vain. The devils cannot harm the servant of Christ when they see he is filled with holy joy. When, however, the soul is wretched, desolate, and filled with sorrow, it is easily overwhelmed by its sorrow or else it turns to vain enjoyments."
(Celano, LXXXVIII, 240)

Who could ever give expression to the very great affection he bore for all things that are God's? Who would be able to narrate the sweetness he enjoyed while contemplating in creatures the wisdom of their Creator, his power and his goodness? Indeed, he was very often filled with a wonderful and ineffable joy from this consideration while he looked upon the sun, while he beheld the moon, and while he gazed upon the stars and the firmament. O simple piety and pious simplicity! Toward little worms even he glowed with a very great love, for he had read this saying about the Saviour: "I am a worm, not a man." Therefore he picked them up from the road and placed them in a safe place, lest they be crushed by the feet of the passersby. What shall I say of the lower creatures, when he would see to it that the bees would be provided with honey in the winter, or the best wine, lest they should die from the cold? He used to praise in public the perfection of their works and the excellence of their skill, for the glory of God, with such encomiums that he would often spend a whole day in praising them and the rest of the creatures. For as of old the three youths in the fiery furnace invited all the elements to praise and glorify the Creator of the universe, so also this man, filled with the spirit of God, never ceased to glorify, praise, and bless the Creator and Ruler of all things in all the elements and creatures.

How great a gladness do you think the beauty of the flowers brought to his mind when he saw the shape of their beauty

*and perceived the odor of their sweetness? He used to turn the
eye of consideration immediately to the beauty of that flower
that comes from the root of Jesse and gives light in the days
of spring and by its fragrance has raised innumerable
thousands from the dead. When he found an abundance of
flowers, he preached to them and invited them to praise the
Lord as though they were endowed with reason. In the same
way he exhorted with the sincerest purity cornfields and vineyards, stones and forests and all the beautiful things of the
fields, fountains of water and green things of the gardens, earth
and fire, air and wind, to love God and serve him willingly.
Finally, he called all creatures brother, and in a most extraordinary manner, a manner never experienced by others, he discerned the hidden things of nature with his sensitive heart, as
one who had already escaped into the freedom of the glory of
the sons of God. O good Jesus, he is now praising you as
admirable in heaven with all the angels, he who on earth
preached you as lovable to every creature.* (Celano, XXIX,
72–73)

The Canticle of Creation, composed so near the end of Francis' life, when he was physically suffering and emotionally
drained, offers a glimpse into the soul of a man whose whole
being was drawn to contemplate the divine mirrored in the reality of life around him. The canticle embraces a cosmic meaning;
Francis is celebrating the gifts of God's creation. Each of the
praises and all of them together also have profoundly spiritual
meaning. Eloi Leclerc, O.F.M. has opened up new understand-
ings of the canticle as a synthesis of personal spirituality and
cosmic mysticism.

According to Leclerc, the sun is the image of the splendor
and abundance of the divine being, the center of life that radi-
ates life. The sun is the image of that sovereign reality upon
which all life depends and from which life is drawn. For the
poetic spirit, the sun shines not only in the heavens but in the
deepest parts of the soul. To enter into communion with Brother
Sun is to open one's being to that wellspring of light, that proph-

ecy of what we are to become, that vision expressing the fullness of God's future. To dialogue with Brother Sun is to probe the meaning of ultimate vocation, ultimate destiny, the New Creation, the Reign of God.

The various cycles of the moon recall the cycles of life, the dying and rising on the journey toward ultimate destiny, the process of becoming. The wisdom of the moon enables one to accept the process of dying and rising and to surrender to the mystery of the night, the unknown, the depths of self, the shadow sides of life. Where the sun symbolized doing, action, vocation, the moon gives focus to substance, being, mystery. Francis' painful eye disease and his own awareness that the end of his life was approaching surely made this reflection on the night most fruitful for him.

The wind evokes images of the Spirit, of great change, conversion, new inspiration, freedom and creativity — apt metaphors for Francis' whole life. His freedom in the Spirit led him to live in a space that was profoundly countercultural and simultaneously prophetic.

Sister Water cleanses and refreshes body and soul. A more powerful symbol of the spiritual life does not exist: baptism, liberation (the Red Sea), new life. Francis was unceasingly the bearer of new life, especially to the most despised. His own liberation toward New Creation was intimately connected with the liberation of the poor ones toward a life of greater dignity.

Brother Fire has the capacity to comfort and to consume. It is a symbol of the movement toward union, of passion, the pathos of love, and suffering. Francis knew the passion of fire intimately; he loved profoundly, embraced suffering, befriended trials, and moved through them accompanied by a God who is love.

Francis sought oneness with Sister Earth; on his deathbed he asked to be stripped naked and placed on the earth. He died in the embrace of Mother-Sister Earth, fully accepting his own finite identity as dust, knowing his absolute limitations.

Finally, Francis embraced the ultimate poverty, the deepest relinquishment of life, the most radical detachment from self — that demanded by Sister Death.

Contemplation: A Way of Living

Thus was the spirituality of the saint of Assisi defined. His way of being was that of profound contemplation: contemplation viewed not as withdrawal from the world, but as entry into its deepest gift—the mystery of life, the presence of God in life and mirrored by life. He moved through life in contemplation, in a fundamental attitude of receptiveness to the Spirit and a primary attunement to the reality around him at all times. His manner of contemplation led to a deeply intentional life; the awareness of God's presence shaped how he lived every moment.

We are called to nothing less. If we follow this call, then who we are and how we are on the journey will be shaped by our contemplation—contemplation born of vigilance to the realities of our world and to God's presence in those realities.

This reflection does not offer a mini "how-to" manual on contemplation. We would be mistaken to see Francis' contemplation as something we must necessarily emulate. The contemplative life may assume distinctive forms based upon the context and upon the nature of the person. However, Francis' amazing communion with the Spirit in all living things makes us almost hungry to uncover and discover the wisdom of contemplation that he embodied.

Contemplation is often equated with going to a place alone, apart, quiet, removing oneself from the world, at least for a short time, to focus on God. Francis' life reveals a much broader concept. Although he often sought out places to pray in solitude, he leads us to see contemplation as a constant, a way of living. Conventional wisdom suggests that the contemplative life is the purview only of introverted or introspective people. Those of us who are extroverts or who do not tend toward quiet reflection generally do not see ourselves as likely contemplatives. Francis, by being both extrovert and profoundly contemplative, again gives the lie to conventional wisdom. He invites all to accept the gift of walking a contemplative path.

The heartbeat of contemplation for Francis was passionate,

consuming desire and willingness to be filled with and led by the Spirit of the Lord. This desire, present explicitly and implicitly throughout his writings, is summarized in his admonition to his followers to "pursue what they must desire above all things: to have the Spirit of the Lord and His holy manner of working" (*Later Rule*, Chapter X:8). To desire the Spirit is to love God. "Let us love the Lord God with all our heart, all our souls and with all our mind and all our strength and with fortitude and with total understanding, with all of our powers, with every effort, every affection, every emotion, every desire and every wish" (*Earlier Rule*, XXIII:8).

Francis shows us that contemplation—birthed in the desire for the Holy Spirit, the love for God—means being awake to, attentive to, and in free and deep dialogue with the Spirit within the self, within others, in all living things, and indeed in all human experience—being present to and receptive to the mystery in all creatures. Indeed, contemplation means acknowledging, accepting, rejoicing in, and living the Spirit as present within life.

Some have said that to contemplate is "to look deeply." Francis' heart looked so deeply that he saw God before all else. For him, life itself was in essence contemplative, an ongoing expression of the Holy Spirit. Thomas of Celano reports that Francis considered the Holy Spirit to be the true Minister General of the Franciscan order.

So we learn from Francis that the contemplative life is not only for people who choose to set themselves apart from the world; nor is it, in the lives of active people, simply reserved for those special moments set apart for attentiveness to God. On the contrary, for Francis "contemplation" was how life was led at all moments. We learn from Francis the reality of *contemplation as a way of being in the world*, not of being removed from the world.

Contemplation and Discipleship

But where do we find authentic "contemplation in action"?

It is to be found nowhere else except in the following of Jesus. Within the framework of discipleship, we can contemplate history as God's history; we cannot do that anywhere else. Discipleship is the authentic locale of contemplation. It is there that we can see what sin and injustice and what love and hope really are. It is there that we can find out who exactly the [Human One] is, the One who preceded us on the same road. Finally it is there we can find out who God is, who keeps opening out history until God eventually becomes all in all (1 Cor. 15:25). (Sobrino, 424)

Salvadoran theologian Jon Sobrino recognizes that discipleship and contemplation are integrally connected in the deepest ways; discipleship is the very ground for contemplation. In other words, we cannot truly know Jesus without following Jesus. Only in the following do we undergo the conversion of eyes, ears, and heart that makes it possible for us to see, hear, and respond to the inbreaking of the Reign of God all around us.

Contemplation makes it possible for us to see the gospel story being reenacted at the very heart of our own discipleship journey. At the spiritual center of our life, we seek to discover in contemplation the gospel story. The dynamic interplay between the gospel story and our own is the subject of contemplation. It is in the contemplative vision that the two stories finally become one.

We know that to be on the discipleship journey means a concrete engagement with history and a struggle against the powers and principalities, those historical forces that thwart and resist the inbreaking Reign of God. Sobrino reminds us that only through contemplation expressed in discipleship can we bear to look upon the brutal chaos of history and to see there anything that promises hope and offers redemption. As Sobrino suggests, it is only through contemplation that we can see history as God's history, see how the Reign of God is hidden in the negative depths of history. It is only with a contemplative vision that the margins of society can be seen not just as places of pain and injustice but of creativity, life, and hope. It is only the contemplative vision that allows us to behold Christ in the face of the leper. Only with a contemplative vision are we able to recognize how we are accompanied through history by Jesus, the Human One who precedes us, opening up history until that moment of final liberation when God becomes "all in all."

Contemplation and Joy

For Francis to be contemplative was a source of great joy. How are we to fathom his unbounded joy and ecstasy? To desire God above all else, to hunger and thirst for God, is an expression of the primal need of the human soul—the need for God. In creating us God created within us the hunger for communion with God. To desire God above all else draws us into communion with God and so is the source of deep joy. Perhaps herein lies insight into Francis' joy.

Carlo Carretto, speaking for Francis, expresses the joy that flowed from contemplation and from seeing God's presence as the unifying force within all life—the presence of God in creatures, in sunlight, in mystery. "For me sunlight was the creature that best betokened God's presence ... Whenever I climbed Mount Subasio in the sunshine I had the feeling that my whole body was penetrated by light—and along with the light, by joy ... Creatures ... contain (God's) presence ... creatures have the ability to lead us little by little to that species of contemplation which ... is the fountain of great joy" (Carretto, 44).

Francis of Assisi must have been a frequent and intimate companion of ecstatic joy—he was as passionate a man as we may encounter. He blindly and fervently followed his love (Lady Poverty, Christ); desired total union with the suffering and the love of God whom he loved beyond and before all else; saw creatures in their amazing beauty and as manifestations of God; prayed, gazed, and wept for hours in front of the crucifix at San Damiano; ran and leapt barefoot in the fields; was aflame with love, mad with love for God, was a "fool for God." Bonaventure says, "He was often taken right out of himself in a rapture of contemplation, so that he was lost in ecstasy" (St. Bonaventure X, 2).

He knew what it was to feel full, overflowing, rich with the intense pleasure of intimate friendship; he experienced the life-giving nature of intimate human relationship in which trust, the sharing of deepest pain and joy, and the bond of the Holy Spirit are assumed.

He drank in the joy of sensuous beauty—the feeling of sunlight on the body, the caress of wind. He must have loved colors, rejoicing in the exquisite colors that adorned the land of Umbria. He must have seen color as another magnificent manifestation of God's love for creation.

So through Francis we see that to love God intensely and to see God in all human experience—the core of Franciscan contemplation—is a source of profound joy.

Contemplation: Subversive Presence

What does contemplative joy as Francis knew it offer to contemporary Christians longing and struggling to be people of justice in a society racked with inequity and oppression? The way in which Francis practiced contemplation opened him to an alternative vision of life, life consecrated to the Reign of God. Contemplation presents a dramatic challenge to life as we live it—a challenge to consumerism, to power or status-seeking, to inequity, to alienation. (This challenge confronts us both as individuals and as a society.) Imagine for a moment if we were to live a contemplative life—seeing and loving God at the core of all people, seeing that "creatures contain God's presence" and are in essence a hymn of praise to God, experiencing ecstatic joy, loving passionately. *To find boundless joy and passionate love in relationship to God's creation is a radical departure from and contradiction to the norms of a consumer society.* If we as a people allowed ourselves to be filled up with joy and love for the created order, we certainly would not destroy the earth, acquire material affluence at the brutal expense of the world's poor, or wage warfare to protect oil supplies. Could we accept homelessness?

Could we fail to protest war? Could we grant the "successful" more respect than the faltering?

If we non-poor Christians were both committed to global justice and open to a fraction of the ecstasy, the love, and the Spirit that Francis experienced, we would be a brilliant and powerful witness to the New Creation. And we would be sustained for the path of discipleship.

Contemplation as a way of living calls into question many of the inequities that we accept in our society. Francis shows us that the contemplative is moved to be a servant to those in need, to be in solidarity with the oppressed, to rejoice profoundly, and to challenge the principalities and powers that create political and economic inequity. We begin to see that contemplation is the fertile soil out of which the "fool of God" is begotten.

Contemplation: Doorway to Compassion

In the life of Francis we see that contemplation gives birth to compassion. (Compassion is not to feel *for;* it is to feel *with* and to be moved to act on behalf of. Compassion, the outstanding characteristic of Jesus' life, means "to have one's guts be torn apart" with feeling.) Conventional wisdom trains us to be dispassionate in the face of suffering multitudes, not to see the enormity of human pain. So shattering and excruciating is the suffering of so many that we run from it with such practiced dexterity that we fail even to notice our own running. To face it would be unbearable; it would paralyze us; it is too excruciating. Yet in some inexplicable way, contemplation opens the door to seeing and to compassion. Is it because contemplation renders our spirit more deeply connected to living things? Is it seeing Christ in the suffering and Christ accompanying the suffering—the sacrament of one's neighbor—that enables us, too, to approach, touch, and suffer deeply with those who suffer? To do so is a tremendous gift. It makes suffering bearable and helps heal the wounds inflicted by it.

And what of that strange mystery revealed so clearly by Francis: that for the contemplative, out of the most enormous physical, spiritual, emotional, or existential suffering can be born perfect joy — pure, crystal, divine. In no place is this more evident than in the Canticle of Creation, composed in Francis' most agonizing moments. Reason cannot explain how, in the face of even the most barbaric evil and excruciating suffering, the divine and gracious Presence may be known, especially for the contemplative whose heart finds God in all moments. Stories speak where reason fails. A telling example can be found in the account of five Franciscans who suffered brutally at the hands of the Nazi SS, singing God's praise through the Canticle of Creation (see Appendix).

Contemplation and the Inner Struggle

Within each of us abides the power for good and for harm, deep-seated passions and energies that may be channeled in life-giving ways or destructive ways. Contemplation is a source of liberation from the negative, crippling dynamics within us — fears, complexes, addictions, desires, hidden wounds, and a false sense of worthlessness.

In Francis we see one who opened himself to the totality of his psyche. He plumbed his own inner depths, the mystery of his soul, the presence of the life-giving and the life-destroying within. Facing and struggling with the dark side of his being through contemplation led to profound inner integration and reconciliation which, in turn, freed him to be reconciled with all of humanity and indeed with all of creation. On one level, the Canticle of Creation is a poetic expression of reconciliation and union between Francis and the totality of his being. Although composed by one who had struggled and suffered intensely, it is filled with lightness and devoid of anxiety. This is the song of a soul finally reconciled with itself and with creation.

Many of us remain enslaved by inner struggles, either by refusing to acknowledge them or by failing to confront and struggle with them. Francis demonstrates a radically different path, a contemplative approach that trusts in God's loving presence even in the midst of inner darkness. He shows us that when, with true humility, in fear and trembling, and in total reliance upon prayer, we face the negative elements within, we will be met there by an infinitely loving God. Walter Wink writes of the power of prayer to bring freedom from the false and crippling sense of worthlessness with which so many struggle: "The kind of prayer of which I speak ... is ... an existential struggle ... against images of worth and value which stunt and wither full human life." If in prayer we aim more to listen to God than to talk to God, then we are blessed by the voice of the one who loves us infinitely and unconditionally. Francis shows us that this encounter with God's love leads both to inner reconciliation and to becoming a reconciling force in the world.

For Francis, fully and humbly facing the struggles within himself was a doorway into a deeper encounter with God. It brought him face to face with the mercy, the boundless love, and the grace of God, which is ever more powerful than sin. Our experience can be the same. As God's beloveds we are the subjects of a love unfathomably magnificent, limitless, and unconditional. Contemplation nourishes an ever deeper awareness of God's love, which in turn grants us the courage to face the aspects of self from which we run and of which we are afraid. God's accompaniment in that confrontation leads to more profound contemplation.

Contemplation and Thanksgiving

Loving God before all else and seeing in all created things a reflection of God—the essence of Franciscan contemplation—called Francis to praise and thank God at every moment in every place, not out of duty or obligation but as a love offering. Francis challenges us to live as though we really believe all that we have and are is divine gift. If we believed all to be gift from God, then for the benefit of all we would share with justice, as did Francis, and we would offer our talents primarily in service.

Francis teaches us in our thanksgiving to look beyond things and circumstances to God, to see the Giver in every gift. "We thank You for Yourself. ... " These simple words open Chapter

XXIII, entitled "Prayer and Thanksgiving," of Francis' *Earlier Rule*. These words invite us to praise our Source regardless of the circumstances in which we find ourselves; for even in the most wretched reality God is. The prayer, "We thank You for Yourself" — frees us from the need to possess and hold on to that which is good; for it reminds us that when the good is gone or changed, the most important gift remains — the gift of God's self. Here again, in his invitation to thanksgiving, Francis leads us to God's foolishness.

Prayer and Contemplation

"Pray all the time, asking for what you need, praying in the Spirit on every possible occasion" (Eph. 6:18).

The contemplative life as modeled by Jesus and by Francis is in one sense a constant prayer: to be attentive to God in all moments, to see the whole world as sacrament is to *be* in prayer. Yet both Jesus and Francis also frequently sought out moments for another form of very personal communion with God. Certainly it would be presumptuous of us to claim much knowledge of these most intimate moments between Francis and God. Yet we can get a glimpse into their nature from the descriptions of Celano and Bonaventure, as well as from the prayers written by Francis. Francis' times of prayer were very powerful, passionate times in which he received comfort, guidance, and revelations of God's wisdom; conversed intimately with his Love, Christ; interceded on behalf of others; and wrestled with the devil. Often he sought out abandoned churches or lonely places in the woods to pray alone. When he returned from prayer he was a man transformed, but sought never to display the fruits of his communion. Francis' biographers show him praying on every possible occasion, casting all of his cares and needs on God through prayer. "All his attention and affection he directed with his whole being to the one thing which he was asking of the Lord, not so much praying as becoming himself a prayer" (Celano, LXI, 95). Prayer helped him to remain attentive to God's presence, to live in contemplation. Francis derived profound pleasure from prayer, his soul in prayer receiving its food, which was God.

For many contemporary Christians, in contrast, not having experienced prayer as life-giving contact with God, it is hard to find reason to pray. Prayer becomes pushed to the wayside or relegated to mealtime, bedtime, and Sunday morning rituals. In fact, most of us are aware only of the form of prayer in which we briefly address God, either alone or in groups, with words, usually of praise or petition. The deeper prayer of Francis, which includes stillness before God, listening to God, and communing fervently with God is largely unfamiliar to us.

Many powerful barriers stand in the way of prayer for Christians today. One is the tendency to think we don't need it. We get along fine without prayer. We have technology, wealth, and power to supply our needs. Prayer seems superfluous, almost superstitious. Another barrier is that we are accustomed to getting results, we expect results, and when we pray we often don't seem to get them. With prayer, it may seem that God does not respond, or that God responds in a way that we do not like, or that we just do not know whether or not God responds. This question of response especially impedes prayers of petition and thanksgiving. We may not want to thank God when "good" things happen because so doing might imply that God is either heartless or powerless in the face of the "bad" things. Perhaps the biggest barrier to prayer is that we don't trust it. We know that prayer won't protect us from excruciating pain; we know that Christians who pray experience torture, agonizing death, and unbearable losses. And finally, at times we simply may feel too exhausted by daily life or too full of despair in the face of human suffering to pray. So why pray?

What response does Francis' life offer to our unspoken "Why pray?" Francis' guide was the example of Jesus, who invites us by his example and summons us by his words to dialogue with God. The gospels portray Jesus as one who prayed deeply. Like Moses, Elijah, the Galilean holy men of his time, and others of the tradition in which Jesus stood, he frequently withdrew in solitude for prayer. "In the morning a great while before day,

he rose and went out to a lonely place and there He prayed"
(Mark 1:35). Jesus in word and deed shows that prayer is essen-
tial to the discipleship journey. For us, as for Francis, following
Jesus leads to prayer.

Finally, to pray as an element of following Jesus is an act of
freedom. It is a stance of freedom from all of the societal forces
that lead many sincere Christians to give up prayer. (Bonaventure describes Francis wrestling intensely with the temptation
not to pray.) It is freedom from dependence upon one's own
motivation to pray. It matters not that we be discouraged,
despairing, or exhausted. Jesus invites us to pray; he offers to
feed us with prayer. Francis knew that freedom: he prayed in
all circumstances—in suffering, in joy, when facing danger, or
in seeing beauty. Prayer offers the freedom to believe in the face
of disbelief. Even when we feel abandoned, or overwhelmed by
the darkness, or believe that our prayer disappears into emptiness, Jesus shows us that the relationship with God is present
even in God's apparent absence. "My God, my God, why hast
thou forsaken me?" Francis joyfully accepted the freedom
offered by the discipline of prayer.

Prayer was, for Francis, essential sustenance. So can it be for
us. How can we possibly hear and respond to the other calls of
Christ without the sustenance of prayer? Without prayer can we
confront violence, the powers that separate us into rich and
poor, the forces that destroy the earth, despair and pain, and
the temptation to sleep while Jesus (and my neighbor) is in
agony? Indeed, for many who have sought to face evil in its
awesome dimensions, we pray because we know that in the end
evil cannot be overcome without prayer! To pray in the face of
evil is to proclaim the New Creation in the moment at hand.

As Francis so clearly experienced, prayer engenders intimacy
between the human person and God. Prayer nurtures the faith
that God knows one intimately and that the initiative for relationship with God lies with God; it is a gift. In praying we trust
that "Before they call I will answer; while they are yet speaking
I will hear" (Isa. 65:24). We are assured that even when we
know not what to pray, "the Spirit expresses our plea with sighs

too deep for words" (Rom. 8:26). When we continue to pray until we hear God, rather than concentrating solely on being heard *by* God, then prayer reveals to us, as it did to Francis, the infused love of God within us and within all creation. To pray as did Francis requires a leap of faith.

By Grace Alone

Franciscan contemplation certainly poses a challenge to the spiritual life of contemporary Christians. Many things take precedence over God in determining our decisions, priorities, and lifestyles. It seems almost impossible to love God before all else, to see the Spirit first in all experience. We may find ourselves backing away from Francis, seeing contemplative living as something that Francis *achieved* and as too far from our reality even to consider it. Yet to do so would be a terrible mistake. Francis did not rise to this state of being. Rather, it was a free gift from God which he accepted. Francis himself reveals that to know the Spirit and to follow Jesus are divine gifts ultimately dependent upon God's grace. In Francis' words, "By your grace alone, may we make our way to you."

Grace — the ceaseless and immeasurable outpouring of God's love for us which offers healing, reconciliation, and illumination — is not at all contingent upon our worthiness of it. Grace is a mystery that the human cannot fathom and even in art, music, or poetry, can only begin to describe as did Francis in the canticle. We must be willing to participate in this mystery, not by comprehension but by faith.

The gifts of loving God and following Christ are given not only to Francis but also to us; we need only accept them. Francis must have understood that amazing truth that God loves us and claims us out of God's pure goodness, not because of any merit or deserving on our part, and that in response to God's love we are called to love and serve God and God's creation; and, furthermore, that God's love for us is far greater and more magnificent than we can imagine. Francis — God's fool — was one who knew profoundly God's grace and responded to it. This divine foolishness is offered to us all.

Trusting in this grace, clinging to the promise that nothing can separate us from God, accepting the free gift of loving presence presents us with a paradox: We can do nothing to earn this gift, yet the paths we choose may serve either to blind us to God's grace or open us up to know it, to accept it gratefully, and to respond. We may be blinded by hearts, minds, and attention so cluttered with fears, activities, and desires that we have no space to receive grace. What, then, are the paths that open us to grace?

First, Francis' conversion process shows us that by seeking to follow Jesus rather than false gods the human being becomes ever more aware of God's love, the power of grace is revealed when one seeks to live in accord with divine will, and the life of discipleship reveals God's love for us. In the words of George MacDonald,

> To shine, we must keep in [Jesus'] light, sunning our souls in it by thinking of what [Jesus] said and did, and would have us think and do. So shall we drink the light like some diamonds, keep it, and shine in the dark ... To let our light shine, we must take care that we have no respect for riches. To treat the poor person with less attention or cordiality than the rich is to show ourselves the servants of Mammon. In like manner we must lay no value on the praise of humans, or in any way seek it. We must honor no person because of intellect, fame, or success. We must not shrink, in fear of the judgment of people, from doing openly what we hold right; or at all acknowledge as a lawgiver what calls itself society, or harbor the least anxiety for its approval. (MacDonald, 81–82)*

Precisely because grace is inseparable from following Jesus, ultimately it is, in Bonhoeffer's words, "costly."

Second, Francis show us that grace is revealed profoundly in the deserts of our lives. Whatever our private or public deserts

---

*We have edited this passage for inclusive language.

may be—agonizing pain, battles with attachments, repentance and conversion, confrontation with evil—the living water of God's grace transforms desert to a garden and brings conversion and a deepened knowledge of God's mysterious love. In the desert lands where the Jewish and Christian traditions were born, living water became and has remained a powerful symbol of God's grace.

We cannot help but remember the desert that Francis experienced after he had received the stigmata. Bleeding, blind, exhausted by forty days of fasting, and his eyes in searing pain, he lay for forty more days in a house adjacent to the monastery of San Damiano. His soul, too, was in agony as he witnessed Christendom, and indeed some within the brotherhood, shunning the values of peace, simplicity, and poverty that he considered essential to discipleship. Celano suggests that conflict raged in Francis' soul and that he prayed not to be overcome by discouragement. It was in this desert that God spoke to him. Francis heard, was filled with utter joy, and composed the Canticle of Creation, that magnificent testimony to grace.

So Francis lights our path with a model of contemplative discipleship born in a trust that the embrace of God's love is ever with us, is abundant beyond our imagining, and is neither initiated by us nor dependent upon us. Understanding that contemplation was given to Francis, not attained by him, and trusting that we are no less beloved of God than was Francis, we too can accept the grace-filled invitation to contemplative discipleship, taste the sweetness of the Spirit in every reality, respond with deeper love, and dare to follow the costly path of Jesus. Indeed we, too, will be fools for God. Instead of backing away from Francis' way as unattainable, we see it as a brother's joyful light.

At the core of Franciscan spirituality is contemplation. To be contemplative is to love above all else the one true God. Out of that love is born the "fool of God." Jesus was the ultimate fool of God. Francis, following Jesus, was the fool. Contemplation leads the fool to see God in the leper, to walk unarmed into the enemy camp, to talk with creatures as brother and sister, to relinquish wealth and privilege, to rebuild the church. This is certainly not, according to the world, a pragmatic path, but one can hardly be pragmatic with a leader like Jesus.

OUR STORIES

• Did your family pray? If so, how? If not, why not?

• When did you first become aware of your own relationship with God?

• Have there been times when that relationship felt very strong? How did or do you nurture it?

• Based upon your own experience how do you define contemplation? prayer?

• Examine your life daily for a month. Describe your spirituality and your prayer life.

SIGNS OF OUR TIMES

St. Augustine once said that God continually tries to give us good things, but our hands are too full to receive them. God offers us the kind of relationship with God's self and with the world that grows in a contemplative life. Yet for most of us our hands are too full to receive this offer. Many features of life in contemporary society draw us away from a contemplative way of living. Our time, energy, and attentiveness go in many directions. Consequently, our attentiveness generally does not focus first on the Spirit within each moment.

"Brainstorm" a list of characteristics and aspects of our lives that draw us away from contemplative living. (For example: a frenzied pace of life, the need for excitement and stimulation, the need to achieve, family, friends, political work, jobs, the desire for more money or nicer things.)

Many things on your list are important and life-giving; many others are destructive at worst, superfluous at best. What would it take for those that are life-giving to draw us toward rather than away from contemplation? What would it take to reduce the influence of those things on your list that are destructive or superfluous?

INVITATION TO RESPOND

Place yourself in a spot conducive to meditation, where you can be safe and undisturbed. Do what feels right to consecrate this space, perhaps by lighting a candle or by playing special music. Be comfortable and begin to breathe deeply at a pace that is natural to you. Allow thoughts to come into your mind without judgment on yourself, but just as easily allow those thoughts to continue out of your awareness, as if you were lying on the warm ground watching clouds go across the sky. Slowly read each of the following prayers based on the Canticle of Creation, and allow yourself to be with each for a time. When you know you are ready, move to the next prayer. (If you are in a group, the prayers can be read successively around the circle.) Listen in your heart to the words of each prayer. Be aware of what images or feelings come up for you. When all the prayers have been read, either in silence by yourself or with the group, make a few notes in a journal about which element of the canticle speaks to you. If you are in a group, allow some time for discussion. When you have thought about the element that seems to be speaking to you, consider how you might continue the dialogue. If it is Brother Sun, plan to be present at a sunrise or sunset in the next week. If it is Sister Water, return to a lake or stream that you have enjoyed in the past. Perhaps it will be some element not included in the canticle. Whichever element you choose, design for yourself a mini-retreat, a meditative encounter with that element of creation as the focus of your contemplation.

When you have decided how to place yourself before this

element, again, go through the steps of allowing yourself to be comfortable and at rest. Breathe deeply. Perhaps you may want to read again the prayer from the canticle or some other reading that feels appropriate. When you have allowed yourself to absorb all the sensations of that element, turn deeply within. What is that element saying to you? Why do you feel you have been drawn to this particular element? What interior reality does this cosmic element represent in you? In spoken words or by journaling, whatever is comfortable for you, carry on a free-flowing dialogue with Brother Sun, Sister Water, or whatever element you have chosen. You may find that the element you have chosen is evoking in you growth and transformation. The element that you choose will undoubtedly change from time to time, as your own contemplative process carries you to new questions of identity and change. Be willing to experiment, to appear "foolish" as you learn more and more how to pray with creation.

Prayers of the Canticle

Now, let us reflect together . . .

Beloved Brother Sun, chosen one of the heavens who brings us each day, we give you thanks. You give bountifully of your heat and light that, doing the work of our days, we may bear fruit and fulfill the promise of our creativity. Brother Sun, you draw our gaze within to that which is deepest and most divine in us. From summer to summer you bless us with the vision of the seasons so that we may know the cycles of our lives and the truth of our unfolding transformation.

Sister Moon and Stars, we thank God for you as you shine in the darkness of night. All praise to God for Sister Moon, who each month passes through all the phases of change. Waxing and waning, you remind us how change occurs in us. In the darkness of ourselves, we are illumined only as we entrust ourselves to the mystery of the night. Sister Moon, so precious and fair, you teach us about death and resurrection. For this we give our thanks.

All praise be yours, God, for brothers Wind and Air, who

bring us all the moods of weather: the evening breezes which caress and storm clouds full of thunder and lightning. Thank you, Brother Wind, for you are the breath of life. Breathe in us, Great Spirit. Blow fiercely if you will. You are the song of all seasons and we give thanks to you.

Sister Water, so transparent and pure, you shimmer with light; you ripple with the wind; you give yourself in service to all things. Teach us how to serve others as you serve us. Teach us your humility so that we might seek out the lowly places as you do, falling freely, joyfully surrendering yourself to gravity's pull. May we give thanks to you, Sister Water, each time our bodies are bathed or our thirst is quenched. May we be baptized by you for joyous service and humility.

All praise be yours, Brother Fire. How beautiful you are as you bring light to night! You dance at our hearths and campfires, soothing us with quiet wonder. Brother Fire, you come to us and ignite our hearts with passion and love. Sometimes you lift us to heights of ecstasy. Other times we know you in depths of trial and suffering. By your touch our souls can be purified. Brother Fire, little brother to the Sun, prepare us for your touch.

Ah, dear Earth, at once our sister and mother, we greet you. Too long have we denied you who give us life. We have been blessed with a dazzling feast at your table. You nourish and sustain us with all good things. We are from you; you have given birth to us. Our very bodies are a gift from you. How can we forget that in every moment our lives depend on you? Teach us never to try to dominate you, but in humility to receive your gifts and care. Help us to heal the painful wounds that we have inflicted on you and on ourselves.

How blessed are those who practice peace, who hunger for justice, who are merciful, compassionate, and quick to forgive. Praise to you, Holy One, for those who have offered us mercy and forgiveness along the way. In gratitude, may we love as we have been loved.

We greet you, Sister Death, so misunderstood and feared. We give thanks for you as well and for the lessons that you teach us if only we will learn from you. You bring us complete poverty and emptiness. You free us from all possession of ourselves. We welcome and give thanks even for you as we entrust our lives without reserve to Being itself.

Epilogue

FRANCIS AND THE FOOLISHNESS OF GOD

Biblical Foundations for the Fool of God

A long tradition of fools exists within the Bible. In the the Hebrew Scriptures we see Jeremiah parading naked in the streets of Jerusalem to drive home a prophetic point. In the New Testament we first catch sight of John the Baptist wearing a camel skin, eating grasshoppers and honey, hanging out in a desert inhabited only by wild beasts, demons, madmen, and an occasional saint. John is a hard one to follow in this mad-cap comedy, but the apostles manage to bring the house down. In the ecstatic moment of Pentecost, they reel like drunks in the gift of the Holy Spirit.

Jesus himself is the head clown of this tradition, the divine fool who, "despised and rejected," calls us to a different way of being and living in the world, a way fundamentally at odds with the accepted norms of behavior. Jesus is the ultimate fool of God, who fulfills a long prophetic tradition and unleashes a message and a new way of life that the world continues to call foolish, irrational, impractical, and dangerously naive.

The apostle Paul heard this invitation and so began to proclaim this message:

For Christ did not send me to baptize, but to preach the gospel, and not with the wisdom of human eloquence so that the cross of Christ might not be emptied of its mean-

167

ing. The message of the cross is foolishness to those who are perishing, but to us who are being saved it is the power of God. For it is written, "I will destroy the wisdom of the wise, and the learning of the learned I will set aside." Where is the wise one? Where is the scribe? Where is the debater of this age? Has not God made the wisdom of the world foolish? For since in the wisdom of God the world did not come to know God through wisdom, it was the will of God through the foolishness of the proclamation to save those who have faith. For Jews demand signs and Greeks look for wisdom, but we proclaim Christ crucified, a stumbling block to Jews and foolishness to Gentiles, but to those who are called, Jews and Greeks alike, Christ the power of God and the wisdom of God. For the foolishness of God is wiser than human wisdom, and the weakness of God is stronger than human strength. (1 Cor. 1:17–25)

Paul called himself and other messengers of the gospel "fools for Christ." And these fools pursued a path of discipleship in the world that led to rejection and ridicule, imprisonment, and, for some like Paul and Peter, even torture and execution by imperial power. Paul called the message of the gospel a stumbling block to Jews and folly to Gentiles. But it was not only the message itself, but also the community that gathered around the message that appeared foolish in Paul's world.

Consider your own call, brothers and sisters: not many of you were wise by human standards, not many were powerful, not many were of noble birth. But God chose what is foolish in the world to shame the wise; God chose what is weak in the world to shame the strong; God chose what is low and despised in the world, things that are not, to reduce to nothing things that are, so that no one might boast in the presence of God. (1 Cor. 1:26–29)

Not many are wise, not many are powerful, but God chose what is foolish and weak to shame the wise and strong; God has chosen what is foolish in the world to bring down the wise. The foolishness of God is God's way of working in the world, using the most marginalized and disreputable as companions in this journey toward liberation. God chose the most unlikely instruments for radical change. It is this community of marginalized people taking on the world with hope, power, and vision that is the most outlandish thing of all.

The Fool in Francis

The tradition of the fool continues throughout the history of the church, springing up in different times and places. We see it in individuals like St. Basil of Russia, who wept with sinners and denounced the czar, who stole the merchandise of dishonest merchants and threw rocks at the houses of the respectable. But nowhere do we see this tradition more clearly than we do in Francis of Assisi.

The worldview of young Francis and his companions was shaped by a romantic vision of the medieval royal court. The courtly ideal for Francis was to become a knight, dedicated first to the service of the king and to a "lady" of the court whose praises he would sing, whose safety and honor he would vouchsafe. It is one of those divine ironies that Francis' sense of vocation shifted from this image of the knight in the royal court to that of the court jester. The fool in the royal court of the Middle Ages was often derided, the source of amusement, the object of mockery. But fools served the court in invaluable ways by mocking the courtly pretensions of power and ambition. Almost everything about the court, even the king, was fair game for the jester because of the tacit agreement that the role of the jester was to remind the court of the limits of its power.

And so Francis became the "fool for Christ," exposing the limitations of the "earthly" court in the light of Christ. We have reflected on the "foolishness" of Francis in stories of his kissing the leper, giving away money, stripping himself naked, always singing, preaching to animals and birds, accepting ridicule and humiliation joyfully, and seeking the suffering of the cross. We have seen Francis walk unarmed into the enemy's camp, take on the momumental task of rebuilding the church, and risk being transformed himself through deep relationships with the other. We have reflected upon his willingness to walk to the edge of security, to lose everything in order to be faithful, and to challenge strongly held cultural, economic, and political norms.

Raoul Manselli, a noted biographer of Francis, has pointed out that it was as fools for Christ that Francis and his community were able to evangelize large crowds, not only in Assisi or in Italy, but throughout Europe and beyond. Because the original Franciscan community was limited by the official church to what was called the exhortation for penance, they were not allowed access to the pulpit to preach sermons. Their church was in the streets, squares, marketplaces and fields. Their congregation was comprised of ordinary people engaged in everyday life; their medium was a combination of exhortation and theater that struck the popular imagination in a way that learned sermons on Sunday failed to do. As fools for Christ, the friars were prepared to accept the fickleness of those they sought to evangelize. As marginalized themselves, the message of the Franciscan community was "totally outside the bonds and limitations of common logic and yet still capable of containing deep, painful, and decisive truths."

The most basic inspiration of the Christian tradition of the fool is identification with Christ crucified, active participation in the poverty, nakedness, homelessness, and humiliation of the Lord. The fool is willing to accept the humiliations, risks, ostracism, rejection, and even violence evoked by faithfulness to the gospel and resistance to evil. We have seen how Francis embodied this identification to the point of bearing in his own body the wounds of Christ on the cross. We have seen how Francis lived this identification with the crucified Christ by living in solidarity with the crucified of the world, the marginalized poor. This is the tradition of the fool expressed as the *via negativa*, the negative way.

But Francis embodied the *via positiva* as well, the positive way in the tradition of the fool, by his unbounded capacity for joy, his sense of ecstatic union with all things, his sensual delight in the created world, his singing of the Lord's song to all creatures; by his sense of the comic and the absurd, his willingness to be the occasion for laughter and amusement, and his gratitude for all things. Francis, as the fool for Christ, united in himself the gospel as both tragedy and comedy.

Foolishness of God at Work and Play in the World

The Franciscan (and divine) "option for the poor" appears utterly foolish in the context of Western civilization today, fundamentally subversive of the thinking, practice, and power upon which the "social order" is rested. Franciscan foolishness turns on its head all that is called wise by the powerful. Franciscan "weakness" transforms the power itself.

Creative appropriation of this foolish way of being in our world requires that we embrace the discipleship journey with abandon. We will experience the subversive joy known by Francis only if we risk embracing the lepers of our day and relinquishing the privilege and wealth that preclude such an embrace. We, too, are invited into dialogue with the ones we know as enemy, with the other, with creation itself, and with our own pain and suffering.

For Jesus and Francis and for ourselves, this foolishness is essentially embodied in the life of the community of believers:

— to relinquish the security of posssessions in a society unable to take risks only makes sense if our ultimate security rests in God;

— to walk away from the familiar and comfortable in order to follow an unknown path of love and service requires the support of cobelievers;

— to believe that we can and must participate in the transformation of the world is best balanced by a loving community that reminds us not to take ourselves too seriously;

— to ask "Why?" and to free ourselves from the ideological captivity of a consumer society is only possible when the road is shared.

The fool in our times honors the Creator in all persons and all things, finds profound joy in the possibility of reconciliation across cultural and racial differences, seeks harmony with the rest of the created order, and is a nonviolent promoter of life.

The fool is in the world but not of the world. The fool finds identity not in that which our society acclaims—appearance, accomplishment, affluence, power, consumption—but rather in the discipleship journey toward God.

The fool knows that we and all created things are sacraments of God. The fool believes in and knows by experience the world of the Spirit.

The fool lives in paradise, ridiculing the powers and principalities, because, with Jesus and Francis, the fool in our times remembers the end of the story, the Reign of God.

Appendix

THE LANGUAGE OF THE SOUL'S NIGHT

The following story from "The Language of the Soul's Night," from Eloi Leclerc, The Canticle of Creatures, *gives powerful witness to Franciscan "foolishness" in our century—a "foolishness" that has enabled life and hope to survive, even in the belly of the beast.*

April, 1945: The Allied armies are penetrating deep into the heart of Germany. A lengthy freight train is moving slowly along the line from Passau to Munich, with thousands of exiles packed into its cars. They have been shut up there for twenty-one days now. Hundreds have already died; hundreds more are at death's door, delirious from hunger. The train started from Buchenwald and has made a long detour through Czechoslovakia and the mountains of Bohemia; now it is heading for Dachau near Munich. Suddenly, incredibly, singing can be heard from one of the cars; it is Francis of Assisi's *Canticle of Brother Sun*! "All praise be yours, my Lord, through all that you have made, and first my lord Brother Sun ... All praise be yours, my Lord, through Sister Earth, our mother."

What can such a song mean in circumstances like these? The men who sang were hardly more than ghosts themselves, surrounded by the dead! What was going on in this railroad car?

Now that we have finished our study of the *Canticle*, we ask the patient reader to let us insert here a few pages of the diary we kept during the time of our deportation from France.

173

We can think of no better illustration of the thesis we have been developing in this book: that Francis of Assisi's *Canticle of Brother Sun* is not simply an expression of esthetic, or esthetico-religious, emotion at the spectacle of nature, but the expression of an experience that takes place in the night of the soul.

Yet as we open this diary, we feel a scruple. Who, after all, can claim to have had an experience really like that of the Poor Man of Assisi? There has been only one Francis of Assisi, and he alone has sung, with identical fraternal feelings, of both the sun and death. Well, we are not claiming to have imitated him, even from afar. But is it not amazing that we were given the grace of singing the praises of the sun while the shadow of death hovered over us?

April 7, evening: Night has fallen, the train rolls on. In what direction? We do not know. One thing is certain: we are on our way—ninety to a hundred men in each car, crouching, crushed against one another, a fellow prisoner between one's legs, like skeletons packed one upon another. The horrible nightmare is beginning. (Could we possibly have thought at that moment that it would last, not three, four, or even five days, but twenty-one days and twenty-one nights?)

No room to stretch out a leg. And we are so exhausted! And so full of despair, too! This very morning, we were still in Buchenwald, waiting for a liberation that seemed very near. We had waited all through the winter, amid hunger and cold, hard work, and death. Many had died. At last, we had survived all that. Then, suddenly, liberation was at hand. It had lifted its head only a few miles away, as real and as powerful as the spring sun that had defeated the long winter. From the hilltop at Buchenwald we could see the flames from the mouths of the American guns. It was only a matter of days now, perhaps even of hours. The cannon were thundering, and hope was leaping in our hearts.

But the SS decided to evacuate a section of the camp. Several columns of prisoners had already set out, under heavy guard on the preceding days. Today it was our turn. With death in our hearts, we walked the few miles from the heights of Buchenwald to the station at Weimar. We were turning our back on hope, this long column of four to five thousand condemned men. Really, we were no longer among the living. Some comrades, their strength drained away, fell during the march, and the SS put a bullet through their heads. In some spots, the path was spattered with blood and brains.

At Weimar station, they put us on board.

Now we are rolling onward into the unknown. Two SS guards to each car. Some cars are covered; others, like ours, still black from coal dust, are open to the sky. A few comrades were able to bring a blanket; luck for them, since the nights are still cold in Germany at this time of the year when winter is barely over. A deathly silence reigns among us. Rocked by the swaying of the train, we sink into a boundless sadness.

Next morning, Sunday, April 8: We stop at a small station. The train stands there all day, then all night. We are forbidden to stand up, even to restore circulation to our legs. We are forced to remain crouching, day after day. For food, a few potatoes and a bit of bread; nothing hot, of course. Meanwhile, a very cold fog descends.

There are people from all over Europe among the hundreds or so packed into our car. From all social classes, too. Most are between twenty and thirty years old, but all look like very old men. Some know why they were arrested and deported: they were part of a resistance movement. Others are there simply because they were caught in a random sweep in Paris or Warsaw or some other city. But we speak as little as possible of such matters. In extreme wretchedness such as this, what is there to know about a man except the suffering that now fills his being? Here the suffering is limitless and everyone shares it. All differences fade away in the face of the common destiny. Lost in this mass of men, there are five of us who are sons of St. Francis.

Monday, April 9: The train starts moving again shortly before noon. While we are under way, the SS relax their vigilance. We take advantage of this to stand for a moment and take a look at the countryside through which we are passing. During the afternoon the train stops in the extensive suburbs of Leipzig, and the SS have those who have died during the journey brought out of the cars. These are quickly and unceremoniously buried beside the track. During the night and throughout Tuesday morning, we continue on eastward. We travel along the Elbe for a while and are only about thirty miles from Dresden. But now the train turns southward.

At this time the SS were probably intending to take us to the concentration camp at Flossenburg in the Oberpfalzer Wald on the Czechoslovakian frontier. For reasons unknown to us they had to drop this idea.

Wednesday morning, April 10: We are at Pilsen in Czechoslovakia. Groups of Czechs immediately gather along the tracks. They are deeply moved at the sight of our striped garments and skeletal figures. They begin to throw bread to us. The SS men fire a few shots at them. The train rolls on slowly and passes under a bridge in the city. Some people who have gathered on the bridge drop food into the cars. We knock each other over trying to get a morsel of bread. More than ever, we are forbidden to stand up, but our hunger is too strong to resist. The train stops at a little station in the countryside, not far from Pilsen. There we are shunted to a siding.

In the evening, they give us a little food: one ration-loaf of bread for ten men. The day ends with the departure of the dead whose number increases each day. The corpses are no long buried beside the track. The corpses are hardly more than skeletons now; they are seized by the arms and legs, shoved upwards, and tipped over into the car.

Next morning, Thursday, April 11: The train stands all day in this little station. In the evening, the dead are removed; nothing else happens all day long. The same thing the next day; we spend all day without food, and in the evening they remove the dead. Life is tragically simplified for us now. We have only one occupation to fill our time: watching others die, while we ourselves wait for death. On the average, two men died each day in each car; that means about a hundred deaths a day for the whole train.

These days spent motionless seem endless to us. But the nights bring a further torment. Alongside the dying, who are at their last gasp, some of the living fight for a bit of space in which to sleep; others go mad and pound their heads against the sides of the car in order to finish their nightmare. Over us, an SS man rains down blows with a club in order to restore quiet. But even all this is not the worst. The terrible, awful thing is to find oneself watching for a neighbor to die and telling oneself that tomorrow there will be more room to stretch out in.

During the night between Friday and Saturday, attempts are made to escape from several cars. This act of despair will cost all of us dear. In the morning, a SS officer climbs into our cars and fires into the mass of prisoners. Two of our comrades are hit; they will spend a long time dying.

Only on Monday, April 16, does the train set out again. We have the impression the SS do not know what to do with us and will be forced to kill us all. But the weather is marvelous. Everything is a call to life: over our heads, a wide blue sky; the larks tumble about up there, drunk on the freedom of space; in the fields men and women are working at the harvest; yonder a few small churches lift up their steeples. The train stops again at evening, on a plateau. Once again we wait, face to face with death. There we are, completely cut off from everything that is going on in the world. Where are the Allies? What is happening in France just now? These big questions seem irrelevant to us now. For many of us, it is already too late.

During the night between Tuesday and Wednesday, the train starts up again. It travels toward the southeast. Now we are entering the mountains of Bohemia. The scene is full of grandeur. From the floor of our car we can watch the forests on the upper slopes. The new light-green foliage of the birches stands out against the dark green of the giant firs. Here and there the gold of flowering bloom catches the eye. Spring is bursting out. Nature, ignorant of what men are doing to each other, continues to produce greenery and flowers once again. From the moist warm earth the sun draws the good smells of a forest in the spring.

In some places the slopes narrow into a rocky, precipitous ravine. Our train with its five thousand condemned men moves slowly through these wild ravines. The idea comes to us that we have been brought there for some barbaric celebration. Then suddenly, fear. Above our heads, over the side of the car appears "the killer," an SS officer. We have called him that because he has already killed several among us. He stares at us the way a bird of prey stares at a nestful of creatures he is going to kill. His rifle is pointed at us; the monster fires into the heap of men. Two comrades are now dying. One has been shot in the mouth. We are all spattered with blood. A terrible anxiety grips body and soul. There can be no doubt now, we feel our hearts jumping wildly, like a bird that has been mortally wounded and flutters around in its own blood, unwilling to die.

We have been traveling all day. This evening the train has halted in a little station at the edge of the Böhmerwald. The railroad bridge across the Danube at Passau has just been cut. We are forced to stay there on a siding several days, six to be exact. Long, terrible days. To crown our wretchedness, the good weather is followed by rain. It falls, cold and steady, for three days and three nights. We are paralyzed by the cold. There is nothing hot for us to eat. Some of us, coming back from removing the dead, have managed to pick up some pieces of wood and a few bricks along the track. On the bricks we light a fire in the car. It's really more of a ghost of a fire. We crowd around it to get dry and warm, but the flame is too weak. Besides, skeletons can't get warm. Most of these days pass without any food at all being given to us, and we must be satisfied with a few dandelions hastily picked beside the track as we return from fatigue duty with the dead.

The dead! There are more and more of them. Many of our comrades die of dysentery; many of exhaustion. Others have contracted erysipelas and are the most horrible spectacle of all. Within a night or a day, these men become unrecognizable; their swollen fiery faces are completely distorted. Delirious with fever, these unfortunates fill the night with their yelling; they scream for water, but in vain. In the morning, their bodies lie stiff in death. Sometimes the corpses remain in the car throughout the day, washed by the pools of water that have formed here and there on the flooring.

These extremities of suffering plunge us into acute anxiety. It is no longer simply the anxiety that grips any living thing as death approaches. Amid our terrible distress there arises in us a strange feeling that eats away at those inmost certainties which till now had sustained us. We have a growing impression that we have been handed over to some blind, savage power. There we are, thousands of men abandoned to hunger, cold, vermin, and death. The human being is completely crushed. Man, whom we had till now believed was made in God's image, now seems laughable: worthless, helpless, hopeless; a being caught up in a whirlwind of forces that play with him, or rather, pay absolutely no attention to him. Among the corpses that lie in the water of the car, eyes turned back, is a companion or a friend. Everything we can see, every experience we must undergo, tells us we are in the grip of an iron law, handed over to the play of blind forces—and that this, and this alone, is reality.

Reality where the Father has no place! Experience that once in your life, and you will never again speak lightly of the "death of God." It is an atrocious experience. When the Father is absent, the Son is in agony. The Son's agony is always due to the Father's silence, the Father's absence. And where can the least sign of the Father be found in this hell? Now we understand the words, "My soul is sorrowful enough to die."

Black night fills our souls. And yet, on the morning of April 26 when one of us is in his last moments and the light has almost left his eyes, what rises from our hearts to our lips is not a cry of despair or rebellion, but a song, a song of praise: Francis of Assisi's *Canticle of Brother Sun*! Nor do we have to force ourselves to sing it. It rises spontaneously out of our darkness and nakedness, as though it were the only language fit for such a moment.

What brings us in such circumstances to praise God for and

through the great cosmic brotherhood? Theories have no place in our utter confusion of spirit; they offer no shelter against the storm. The only thing that remains and is priceless in our eyes is the patience and friendship this or that comrade shows you. Such an act by someone who, like yourself, is immersed in suffering and anxiety, is a ray of light that falls miraculously into the wretched darkness that envelops us. It re-creates you, makes you a human being once again. Suddenly we learn all over again that we are men. And when such an act of friendly help has been done to you, you in turn are able to do it for another and thus respond to the reign of brute force with a freedom and love that bear witness to another kind of reality. . .

At such a moment, astounding though it seems, we experience wonder before the world; we experience the sacred in the world. Such an experience is possible only in extreme deprivation of soul and body. Only in utter distress and need can we fully appreciate a mouthful of bread, a sip of water, a ray of sunlight, and now and then, like a visitor from another world, the warm greeting of a passerby. The tiny drops of rain that tremble on the telephone wires in the evening light after a storm are filled, to the selfless eye, with boundless innocence. And the broad rain-washed heaven shows us — how luminous, how pure it is! All these lowly things that we can contemplate from the floor of our car are not the result of passing chance. They speak sweetly to the soul.

Where do they come from, this purity and innocence that suddenly lay hold of us through these humble realities? Whence the limpid radiance that bathes the world but is perceptible only amid extreme poverty? How innocent things are. Do you smile? Yet this experience can be matched by no other. Nietzsche said: "One must . . . have chaos in oneself to be able to give birth to a dancing star." We certainly have not been spared chaos. Devastation is everywhere, around us and within us. History has swept like a cyclone across our lives. And yet, over this heap of ruins, there now shines "the great evening star of poverty."

Because this vision was given to us, we were able, on an April morning somewhere in Germany, to gather round our dying brother and sing of the sun and the stars, the wind and the water, the fire and the earth, and also of "those who grant pardon for love of you." "When he died, so light as to be nameless," there was no flight of larks overhead, but a supernatural peace had filled our hearts. That evening we carried his body away, accompanied by blows from the SS who felt we were not moving quickly enough. His was the last death in our car.

Bibliography

Boff, Leonardo. *Saint Francis, A Model for Human Liberation* (New York: Crossroad, 1984).

Bread for the World Institute on Hunger and Development, *1992 Hunger Report* (Washington, D.C., 1992).

Brown, Raphael, ed. and trans. *The Little Flowers of St. Francis* (New York: Image Books, 1958).

Carretto, Carlo. *I Francis* (Maryknoll, NY: Orbis Books, 1982).

Holland, Joe and Henriot, Peter. *Social Analysis: Linking Fatih and Justice* (Maryknoll, NY: Orbis Books, 1983).

Jörgensen, Johannes. *St. Francis of Assisi* (New York: Image Books, 1955).

Kavanaugh, John. *Still Following Christ in a Consumer Society* (Maryknoll, NY: Orbis Books, 1991).

Keen, Sam. *Faces of the Enemy: Toward a Psychology of Enmity* (San Francisco: Harper & Row, 1985).

Leclerc, Eloi. *The Canticle of Creatures: Symbols of Union* (Chicago: Franciscan Herald Press, 1977).

Lilburne, Geoffrey. *A Sense of Place: A Christian Theology of the Land* (Nashville, TN: Abingdon, 1989).

MacDonald, George. *Life Essential*, Rolland Hein, ed. (Wheaton, IL: Harold Shaw Publishers, 1974).

Manselli, Raoul. *St. Francis of Assisi* (Chicago: Franciscan Herald Press, 1988).

Myers, Ched. *Binding the Strong Man: A Political Reading of Mark's Story of Jesus* (Maryknoll, NY: Orbis Books, 1988).

Presbyterian Eco-justice Task Force, *Keeping and Healing the Creation* (Louisville, KY: Committee on Social Witness Policy, Presbyterian Church, U.S.A., 1989).

Shaheen, Jack G. "Our Cultural Demon—the 'Ugly' Arab," *The Washington Post*, August 19, 1990, Outlook Section.

Sobrino, Jon. *Christology at the Crossroads* (Maryknoll, NY: Orbis Books, 1978).

St. Bonaventure. "Major Life of St. Francis" in Habig, Marion, ed., *St. Francis of Assisi: Writings and Early Biographies*, English Omnibus of the Sources for the Life of St Francis, 3rd. rev. ed. (Chicago: Franciscan Herald Press, 1973).

Thomas of Celano. *St. Francis of Assisi: First and Second Life* (Chicago: Franciscan Herald Press, 1963).

Wink, Walter. "On Not Becoming What We Hate," *Sojourners* (November 1986).

Wink, Walter. "The Transforming Power of Nonviolence," *Sojourners* (February 1987).